Performance Puppy

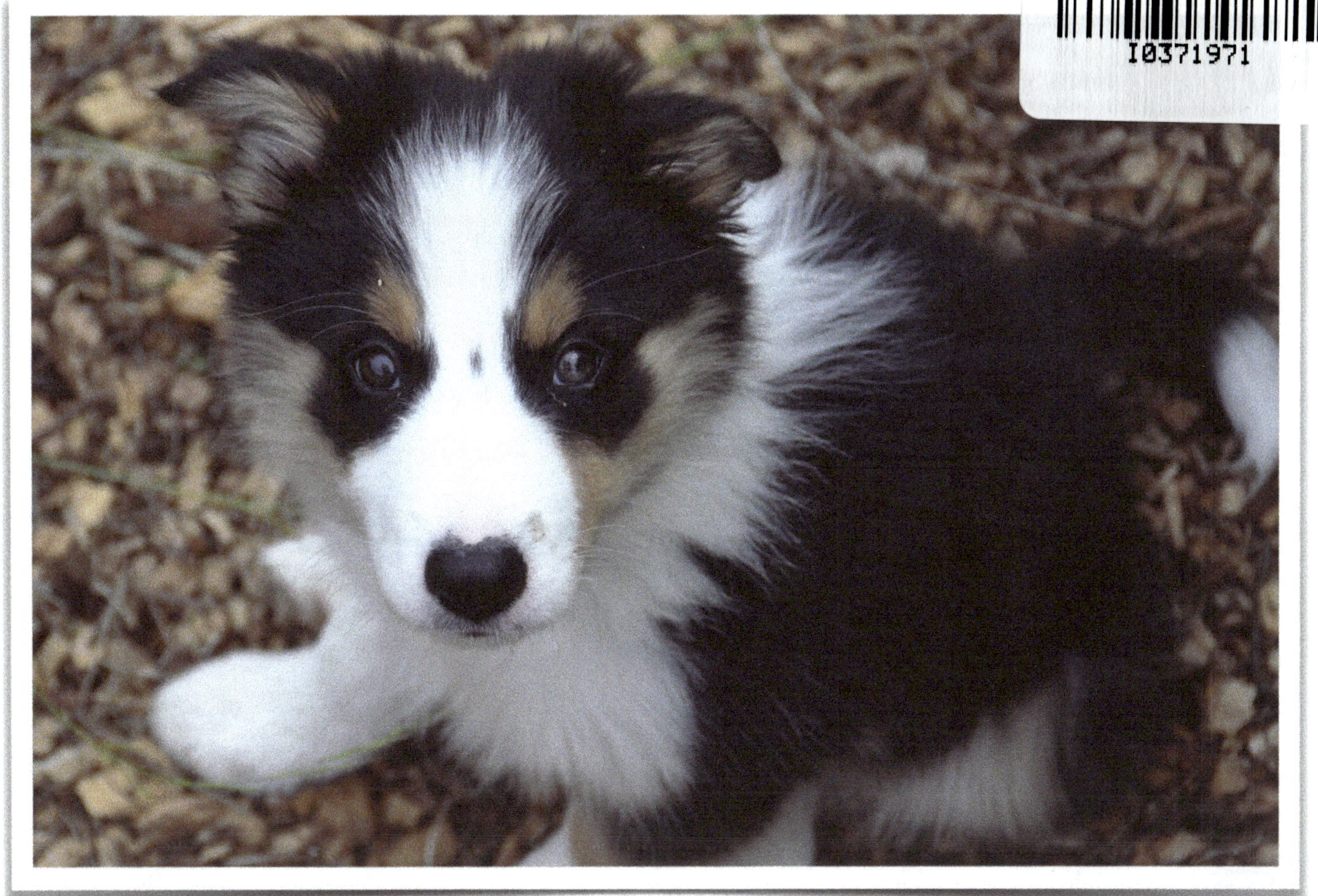

s

The Building Blocks For
Success With Your Next Canine Superstar

By Daisy Peel and Anna Hinze

PERFORMANCE PUPPY ABCs

Copyright © 2019, 2020 by Daisy Creative, LLC
Written and edited by Daisy Peel and Anna Hinze

Website: **https://www.performancepuppyabcs.com**
All elements designed by Daisy Peel

Independently Published by Daisy Creative LLC
27494 S Gard Rd
Mulino, OR 97042

Trademarks: All service marks, trademarks, and product names used in this publication belong to their respective holders

Second edition
First printing December 2020
ISBN 978-1-7362115-1-9
Library of Congress Control Number: 2020923325

All rights reserved. Printed in the United States of America. No part of this book may be used or reproduced in any form or by any means electronic or mechanical, including photocopying, recording, or by any information storage or retrieval system, without the prior written permission of the author, except in the case of brief quotations embodied in critical articles and reviews and certain other noncommercial uses permitted by copyright law. For permission requests, write to Daisy Peel at **daisy@daisypeel.com**.

This book is available at special quantity discounts for breeders and for club promotions, premiums, or educational use. Write for details. The information in this book is complete and accurate to the best of our knowledge. All recommendations are made without guarantee on the part of the authors or Daisy Creative, LLC. The authors and publishers disclaim any liability with the use of this information.

PERFORMANCE PUPPY ABCs

We hope that you enjoy the material in this text, and that the training is fun and educational for you and your puppy! A lot of thought and effort went in to producing this content, and we'd love to hear from you regarding how the training is going! You can contact us using the contact us form at **https://www.performancepuppyabcs.com**. If you purchased this course at **https://www.performancepuppyabcs.com**, remember that there is video and audio for each lesson in the text, as well as a comment section where you can share your training experiences with your puppy, as well as the opportunity to get feedback from the authors.

Finally, thank you for your purchase, and for supporting the work that we've done to put this content together for you! We wish you and your dog many happy training sessions together!

~ Daisy and Anna

PHOTO CREDITS

Photos from **freepik.com**, Daisy Peel or Anna Hinze, unless otherwise credited.
Alex Bereuter, page 102
Tessa Bornemann, pages 3, 16, 19, 21, 23, 30, 45, 48, 51, 65, 71, 81
Johanna Lohr, page 56
Kim Rieger, pages 73, 84

PERFORMANCE PUPPY ABCs

About The Authors - Anna Hinze

ANNA HINZE lives, trains, and competes in Germany, where she instructs students on a daily basis, in addition to teaching seminars throughout Europe. Anna enjoys teaching both novice handlers as well as students who aspire to be on a national team themselves. She teaches in Europe, the USA, and around the world, in addition to teaching online classes. Anna competes with Border Collie May, born in 2011, and Shetland Sheepdog Take, born in 2017. She has represented Germany successfully at different international events in Europe and the USA, including winning the prestigious European Open Team competition in the Large category with May in the summer of 2019.

This book will give you an insight on the first year of the life of Anna's puppy Take. Learn about the behaviors and tricks she taught Take, and use them as a guideline to what you want to teach your own puppy! Feedback is available from Anna in the online course that accompanies this book at **www.performancepuppyabcs.com**

Learn more about Anna Hinze at www.agilitycampus.com

PERFORMANCE PUPPY ABCs

About The Authors - Daisy Peel

DAISY PEEL is known globally as a leading instructor and competitor in the sport of dog agility. She has represented the USA internationally over a dozen times, across three continents, with multiple dogs and has medaled on the international stage. Daisy has also won five National Championship titles, with two different dogs.

Daisy is also recognized globally as an instructor. Her students excel at the top levels in multiple North American agility venues, and have been selected to represent their countries at international events as well. Daisy teaches students around the globe, in person and through her Online Classes and The Agility Challenge, and she is dedicated to helping people enhance their agility experience through better training, handling, and mastery of their mental game.

You'll benefit from Daisy's experience training **four** dogs to World Championship competition levels with all the information in this book! Follow along, and set the tone to dance together on the agility field, as partners highly attuned to one another, with either your current or your future puppy!

Learn more about Daisy Peel at www.daisypeel.com

PERFORMANCE PUPPY ABCs

TABLE OF CONTENTS

Foreword And Introduction 1
Thoughts On How You'll Spend Your Time With Your Puppy 3
No Potty, No Play 6
Reward Charts 9
Recalls To Heel 11
Look At Me! Look At Me! 16
Follow The Food 19
Beginning Name Recognition 21
Baby Nose Bop 23
Voluntary Restrain Or Collar Grab 25
Put On Your Collar 27
Running Is FUN 30
Beginning With Boxes 32
Beginning Red Light, Green Light 34
Beginning Red Light, Green Light - Food Bowl Manners 36
Laying On Your Side 38
Accepting Boundaries 40
The Dog Door 43
Chase The Handler 45
Recalls From Food/Toys 48
Recalls With Distractions 51
Beginning Balance Board 54
Navigating Nature's Obstacles 56
Beginning Manners Minder 58
Beginning Rear Foot Targeting 60
The Two Toy Game - Get The Live Toy 63
The Two Toy Game - Beginning Retrieve 66
The Two Toy Game - Adding Motion To A Retrieve 69
Racing To The Toy 72
Send To Dead Toy 74
Flirt Pole Fun 77
1 Minute Motivation 79
Come To My Side 82
Stay With Me 85
Leg Slap 88
Where's Your Nose? 91

PERFORMANCE PUPPY ABCs

Crawling Backwards 93
Walk On My Feet 95
Turning Left & Right 97
Back Up 100
Mirror Shake / Wave 103
Four Feet In The Box 107
Go To Your Mat 110
Chill On Your Mat (Beginning Stay) 114
Recognize Your Name (Testing Stay) 117
Put Your Toys Away 119
Circling A Cone 122
Ipsilateral (Side Foot) Targeting 128
Discriminating Behaviors 130
Tug Think Tug 132
Listening When Aroused 134
Conditioning For Puppies 136
Transferring Left & Right to Wings 137
Testing Understanding Of Left & Right 140
The Bang Game 143
Introducing The Tunnel 146
Turning Away To A Tunnel 149
Bypassing A Tunnel 152
Final Thoughts 155
About This Book 157

PERFORMANCE PUPPY ABCs

PERFORMANCE PUPPY ABCs

Foreword And Introduction

So many of you, like me, want to make sure you "get it right this time" when it comes to your upcoming performance puppy. There can be a lot of anxiety, worry, and stress. Fear that we will mess up our puppies. Anxiety that we will misstep and not realize it until the "bad" behavior is ingrained and can't be fixed. Are we using the right food? The right toys? Is your puppy in her crate enough? Out of her crate enough? So many sources for worry. So many chances passed by to just ENJOY our puppies.

OK, so, sure, some guidance is great. Having checklists and protocols is great. AND, I intend to provide those, right here in this book. But before you start digging in to the rest of this book, getting all worried about timelines, deadlines, closing windows, missed opportunities, and the like, I just want to say….**STOP. Take a deep breath. Look at your**

Chispa, upside down, sleeping in her crate

PERFORMANCE PUPPY ABCs

puppy, and smile. It's gonna be ok. I just did that, while writing this, and this is what I saw:

There's a LOT to be covered, to be sure. But there are only so many training minutes in each day, and there is only so much room for food in your puppy's tummy, and so much energy for playing. So all of these things take time, and how to SPEND that time is more important really than the end result. I can be exhausted and stressed and breathe a sigh of relief when finally SOME sign that I DID IT comes my way, or I can just enjoy each moment as it rolls by, try to keep track of what I've done so far so I don't duplicate my efforts, jot down some sloppy lists on a piece of mail (I often make lists on whatever piece of paper happens to be available!), and try to avoid worrying too much.

~ *Daisy*

Thoughts On How You'll Spend Your Time With Your Puppy

What to do first?

When getting a new puppy, most of us can't wait to get started on all the fun games and training that there is to do. After all, puppies are a blank slate and we are eager to teach them tricks and skills that will be useful for their lives as performance dogs. However, it is most important to socialize your puppy during the first couple of months with you.

It is during this crucial developmental period, that your puppy will make associations for life. Socialization does not only include other dogs and people, but also as many different situations as you can think of. The more new situations your puppy experiences, the more relaxed she will be when being exposed to potentially stressful situations later in life. For that reason I encourage every puppy owner to spend at least as much time on exposing their puppy to new experiences, as on training.

Creating socializing experiences

Before getting a puppy, I sit down and make a list of experiences that I would like my adult dog to be able to cope with easily. Think of all the things your puppy will do during his life. Will she travel with you by car, bus, train or plane? Will she be around kids, elderly people, disabled people? Will she be with you in crowds of people? Will she come downtown with you and take city trips? Go on the underground train, take elevators or escalators? Will she be around other animals like horses, cattle or chickens? Will she come to a restaurant with you or into a shop?

These are only a few examples. For each situation listed, there will be different stimuli that your puppy will need to learn to be comfortable around. For example, if your puppy is going to take a train ride with you, she should be cool with luggage carts, suitcases being wheeled by, pigeons flapping their wings, crowds of people, loud trains passing by, being carried up an escalator or taking an elevator, being picked up and carried on the train, movement of the train floor underneath her, staying in a bag or on a mat while people walk by and all kinds of strange people that one might encounter in public.

The stress of all these stimuli on a dog should not be underestimated! It is crucial to introduce your puppy to as many stimuli as possible early on, so that she will be able to cope with potentially stressful situations later in life. Give your puppy plenty of time to take all the stimuli in. She will gain confidence from every situations she has mastered. Let her watch from afar if she is insecure and let her move closer at her own pace.

Make your own list

Take a few minutes to make your own list with experiences you deem important for your puppy. Think about how to create such experiences for her without overstimulating her. For example, if you want your puppy to get used to different people, take her to a nursery home and hang out in front of it. Maybe you can even take her in. Now your puppy has the chance to observe people in wheelchairs, people with walking aids or crutches and people walking in a 'strange' manner.

If your puppy is doing really well with all the stimuli and is relaxed, try some of the easier games from this book in the new environment. Start to take your training on the road early on, so your puppy understands to generalize behavior!

~ *Anna*

No Potty, No Play

OBJECTIVE

Until your puppy can reliably relieve herself using the dog door at my house, she'll be under a "no potty, no play" restriction. Even if I'm under a time crunch and REALLY really want to play with her or do a bit of training, it's a no potty no play situation. This may mean that "no potty no play" IS the behavior that we work on. But, this is often the case with training - we start off with the intent to train one behavior, only to realize that we need to switch gears and work on something else instead.

What to do

- First, grab a kibble or two, and then head to your puppy's crate. Open the crate door and reach your hand inside to offer a cookie to your puppy, to help teach your puppy not to bolt through an open crate door. Close the door while your puppy is eating the kibble. Repeat a couple of times and then open the door, say ok, let your puppy come out, and give yet one more kibble.
- Then, head for the door as fast as possible. First, carry your puppy ALL the way to the potty spot. Then, carry your puppy MOST of the way and let her take those last few steps on her own. Let her travel on the ground on her own a little more and a little more each time, until she can run along side you from the crate door to the potty spot with the whole way. Make sure there are no other dogs or toys as distractions in her path first.

How to cue

- DON'T SAY GO POTTY until your puppy is ACTUALLY PEEING OR POOPING. This is at present a word association game, she doesn't KNOW what GO POTTY means. Repeat "go potty", and "good girl" while she's doing the deed, praise highly after, and give a kibble or two, or play with a toy, whichever she prefers.
- No potty, no play - pack her back up if she hasn't pottied, put her back in her crate, offer her food and/or water to push things along, and try again in a few minutes. If she's pottied, then…play!

Tips to remember

Puppies need to potty after they've had a nap, after they've had a meal, and after any stretch of a few minutes of excessive movement (playing, running around, etc.). Predictable, so use it to your advantage to teach a strong association between the words "go potty" (or whatever words you want to use) and the actual act of going potty.

I'm not in any hurry to consider potty training finished, and in fact, I almost never even bother to SAY "go potty" even with my adult dogs, unless I'm pretty darned sure there is a reasonable chance they have to go. AND, if I see them in the act of peeing or pooping, I will absolutely take the time to say "go potty" as they are doing their thing, to keep that word association strong with the behavior.

The "no potty, no play" guideline holds over throughout the life of your puppy as well. I mean, honestly, before I engage in agility fun with my adult dogs, *I* make sure to go potty

PERFORMANCE PUPPY ABCs

myself! We're not so different from our dogs; after we rest, after we eat, and after activity, what's the first thing WE usually need to do? Yep, you got it.

So, consider the no potty, no play guideline a wise one to follow not just for your puppy, but for all of your dogs, and don't forget to take care of your own needs prior to having a bit of fun with your puppy :)

Reward Charts

OBJECTIVE

While one person might enjoy a piece of chocolate after a long day of work, someone else might prefer watching TV at night as a way to reward themselves. Different people are motivated by different factors. Just like humans, dogs also have individual preferences when it comes to what they view as a reward. In the first few days with your puppy, you should take note of what she enjoys, so that you can use appropriate rewards. Are there certain types of treats she likes more than others? Which is her favorite toy? What is her favorite game? Tugging? Retrieving? Chasing?

Pay attention to her preferences.

Top Ten Rewards

In order to help you with figuring out what your puppy likes, we recommend to make a top ten list of rewards. Consider more than food and toys. Does your puppy like you to make funny noises? Chase after you? Snuggling with you? Being allowed to chase after another dog or being allowed access to a certain area of the house? All these things can serve as rewards.

What to do with your list?

Once you have created your top ten rewards, be smart about which reward to use for which exercise. Exercises that require your puppy to be in a stationary position are at first best rewarded with something that is lower on the list. Exercises that require action and fast movement are better rewarded with something higher up. If your puppy is going through a period in which she finds it difficult to focus, or if you are working in a highly distracting environment, chose a reward from the top of your list, to maintain her interest. Check your list regularly. As your puppy develops, you might discover that her preferences change. Toy drive, for example, tends to get stronger as puppies mature.

Building Value for Rewards

You might notice that there are certain rewards that you would like your puppy to crave, but she doesn't. For instance, a certain type of training toy or her regular food. Note these rewards down, but not in your top ten list. It is important to only use rewards that your puppy actually finds rewarding. You should never have to force a reward onto your puppy. However, as time goes by and your puppy develops more desire for working on tricks, as well as drive to chase after toys, you can try to add in your preferred rewards and see if your puppy will accept them. Once you have created enough desire in your puppy to work with you, she will be much more likely to enjoy rewards that she previously didn't.

Recalls To Heel

WHY RECALLS TO HEEL SHOULD BE VIEWED AS A WAY OF LIFE, RATHER THAN AN AGILITY BEHAVIOR

Recently, while teaching a seminar, I taught a session on foundation/fundamentals. These sessions can often go in a variety of different directions depending on the dogs that are present, and this one was no different. One of the students had a puppy just a few weeks older than your puppy at the time, Chispa. Another student had a dog that was about a year and half; quite a spread. "Recalls to Heel" was on the list of things to do, and it's a FUNDAMENTAL behavior in my mind, but also, a super BORING behavior to train.

When I say "recall to heel", I mean a recall as taught in **Mastering Jumping Skills**, a book written by Linda Mecklenburg. It's a skill that does reward your dog for coming to the handler, but it's the HOW that is important. And, frankly, the HOW is applicable to herding, obedience, and life in general. The recall to heel is meant to teach your dog to come to a halt using her rear end (and not just her front end!). No crashing in to anything with the front feet while the rear end swings about. Being able to stop nicely with the front and the rear makes for a nice, sudden stop, like a quarter horse.

What I DON'T want is for your puppy to be stopping or moving in any way that will result in something like the image at right!

So at this seminar, I've got this group of inexperienced dogs, the youngest being 14 weeks. Obviously, the 14 week old puppy isn't going to be able to do all the exercises. BUT, recalls to heel? YES, absolutely, and here are some of the reasons why:

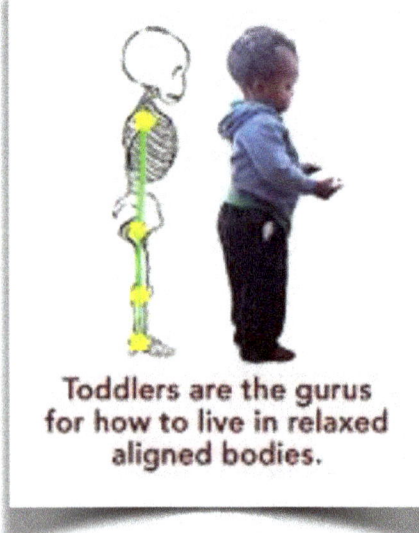

Toddlers are the gurus for how to live in relaxed aligned bodies.

Your puppy can probably already do it

Have you ever noticed how little kids, toddlers, can sit with the most amazing posture? They also STAND with the most amazing posture.

When asked what I do to CORRECT some of the problems dogs have with the recall to heel, I was at a loss for words. I know all the things you **can** do, and I teach all of those things, but since puppies are high on my mind, I realized the best answer was to *never let those issues develop*. This led in to the question of "do I reward if the dog does it wrong?" Again, ideally, I don't want to be in a position to HAVE to withhold reinforcement with this one - I don't want to NOT reward my dog for coming to me, after all! I'm going to work hard to create a situation where I know your puppy WILL stop nicely as she comes to me, so I don't have to decide I don't want to reward her because I don't like HOW she came to me. Leaning in to her, shifting my weight, adjusting my own posture slightly so that she shifts back and comes to a stop using her rear end nicely.

Puppies, like toddlers, already HAVE good "use" of their bodies. Correcting people's posture problems is a HUGE industry - so many of us engage in ways of moving about in our world, including sitting, that are NOTHING like the way we sat, stood, walked, or ran when we were toddlers. Of course, we are much more coordinated, but our posture is typically much worse, and that poor posture typically leads to all sorts of problems.

Puppies, like toddlers, already seem to possess the ability to move nicely through their worlds. Sure, they're floppy and not coordinated. BUT, they can stop with their rears square behind their fronts. They can come in for a recall and they already DO it. It's we as handlers/owners who start to promote poorer "use" of their bodies, either through what we allow to happen in the house, at the park, OR, in formal training.

The goal of ANY training is to CAPTURE the behavior, REWARD it, and GROW it.
Puppies already HAVE this behavior -
we just have to capture, reward, and grow it!

This training is not the most exciting stuff

Another reason to start working on recalls NOW (aside from the notion that right now there's lots of GREAT behavior to capture, reward, and grow) is that it's not super exciting. But, I can honestly say, I NEVER have recalls to heel on my to-do list.

Recalls aren't something I decide to start

working on. They're not something that I put in my training book or calendar. It's just the way I want my dogs to come in to me - ALWAYS. From the very beginning. You'll never hear me say "oh I worked on recalls today". The only time I've formally worked on recalls as an exercise that I can remember (assuming I did this early on when I was just learning) was when I was filming them with Chipper for the Mastering Jumping Skills Foundation Flatwork class. I just don't think it's exciting enough to be working on during a formal training session. If I just make it part of the way we interact, ALWAYS, I don't need to WORRY about making it exciting - it's just how we dance together.

This isn't an agility skill, it's a LIFE SKILL

As I mentioned before, I want my dogs to ALWAYS be coming in nicely to me, stopping with their rear ends underneath them, not just in agility!! Nothing makes me cringe more than seeing dogs running around with no regard to how they're going to STOP. I start seeing dollar signs in front of my eyes, and vet bills. I don't want them running in to me, or each other, or the walls, or trees, or anything. I don't want them slipping and sliding through life. I'm pretty careful to not engage in behaviors such as coming in to me for a toy, grabbing the toy, and swinging off of it. Obviously my dogs run around, and obviously I play games with them that include toys. I just try to be constantly aware of what good "use" is, and encourage and promote it.

Look At Me! Look At Me!

I want to take a few moments to discuss the idea of our puppies needing to constantly look at us. WHY is this? Yes, we want to be the center of our puppy's world. And yes, we want them to look to us for their needs. For safety, for security, for sustenance, and for FUN. But do they need to constantly be STARING at us in order to prove to us that they are in fact viewing us as pivotal in their lives?

I'm going to suggest…NOPE.

ATTACHMENT AND BONDING

I want to spend a bit of time on the concept of attachment and bonding - it's a fascinating subject that I think applies in so many ways to our DOGS. Check out this link for some information on what is called "The Strange Situation" experiment: **https://www.simplypsychology.org/mary-ainsworth.html**

Basically, there are four responses a child can have in what is called "The Strange Situation" experiment, depending on how securely or INsecurely they are attached to their parent or caregiver.

Read through those four responses in the link on the previous page. Now, apply this situation to your puppy. You're in an environment, your puppy knows you're there, you make everything seem ok, and your puppy is exploring its environment. If you reenact the strange situation experiment, how does your puppy react? More importantly, how do YOU react? Are YOU reacting in this situation in a way that indicates a secure attachment?

It's not entirely farfetched to put forward that on OUR part, there is that feeling of, "Oh my God, your puppy doesn't love me, your puppy is ignoring me, just LOOK, your puppy won't even come to me, I'm a failure" and so on and so forth, when our puppy is confidently exploring her environment, looking happy, while we just stand there, feeling a little abandoned. Come on, you KNOW what I'm talking about.

But what if we considered this situation from the point of view of attachment and bonding theory? That if WE have done our job as "parents" correctly, then our puppies are MORE likely to feel brave exploring their environments? That, if our puppies know we've got their backs, they are MORE likely to be that puppy that can work the crowd, seemingly ignoring us. Our puppies are SECURE. And, don't we want that?

Now, obviously, we'd like to know that our puppies ARE secure. And when your puppy is secure in her environment, how do you KNOW she's paying attention to whether or not YOU, the center of that security, are there? Read through "The Strange Situation"

experiment again at that link, and recreate it! See what happens in that situation with your puppy instead of a small child. AND, note your OWN responses to your puppy when you return to the room after an absence. Are YOU secure in your attachment to your puppy?

There are some consequences to teaching a puppy to constantly look at you to the exclusion of being able to investigate its environment. Keeping a puppy or a dog from being able to check out its situation is not likely to make that dog feel MORE secure in their environment. And if we, as owners, are begging for that eye contact and not letting our dogs explore, WE are not demonstrating the behavior of a creature in a securely attached relationship with another creature. It actually saddens me a bit to be at a show and hear a competitor saying "look at me, look at me, look at me" constantly to their dog or puppy, who is desperately trying to figure out what is going on around them so that they can decide if they are safe enough to be comfortable. Both in this situation strike me as insecure as to the status of their relationship with one another, and to their environment.

There are a lot of directions to go with this line of thinking, but since, in this puppy course, we're keen to address these sorts of PHILOSOPHICAL topics in addition to some training topics, we'll leave you on that note to ponder, and hopefully join the discussion if you're taking the class online, and RESPOND!

Follow The Food

OBJECTIVE

You'd think that puppies came learning to eat food from the hand, and they DO seem to pick it up quickly, but this is a simple behavior I want to remember to address. There's nothing formal about this, and there's no determinant of "success"; I just want your puppy to be able to follow my hand when I have food in it (yes, I lure, eek!), and I also want your puppy to be able to visually track a piece of food I've thrown.

I just use kibble for this - at this stage, your puppy is getting all of her food from my hand or from a food puzzle (kong), and so right now, she thinks that kibble is the best treat ever! With any luck, she'll continue with that belief, and be a raptor for kibble, as are all the rest of my dogs :)

What to do

- Hold a piece of food or two in your hand and move your hand in front of your puppy's face, slowly enough that your puppy can follow it, first with just her head, and then with her whole body, taking a few steps after it
- Hold a piece of food, make sure your puppy can SEE it, and toss it, just a few inches. Make a show of tossing it, not too quickly, so your puppy sees it being tossed, sees it landing, and moves toward it to eat it.

Tips to remember

Make sure you're using food your puppy wants to eat, AND make sure the food is easily spotted both in your hand, in the air, and on the ground! Keep the distance you toss the cookie short - just a few inches! And, don't go overboard, just a few cookies is fine (less than TEN!).

Beginning Name Recognition

OBJECTIVE

Once your puppy is able to follow a piece of food that has been tossed a few inches away, you can start the process of teaching her that a certain sound (her name!) means something good is happening in my direction. You're looking for a head turn toward you with this little behavior, and it's a natural progression from "FOLLOW THE FOOD" because it resets your puppy to look away from you for the NEXT thrown piece, which resets your puppy to look BACK to you when you make the NAME sound :)

This and FOLLOW THE FOOD are part and parcel of the same thing, really; one follows from the other organically.

What to do

- Hold a piece of food or two in your hand and move your hand in front of your puppy's face, slowly enough that your puppy can follow it, first with just her head, and then with her whole body, taking a few steps after it
- Hold a piece of food, make sure your puppy can SEE it, and toss it, just a few inches. Make a show of tossing it, not too quickly, so your puppy sees it being tossed, sees it landing, and moves toward it to eat it.
- Just as your puppy is finishing up eating her piece of food, cheerfully call her name, and when she turns her head back toward you, reward, and repeat.

Tips to remember

Make sure you're using food your puppy wants to eat, AND make sure the food is easily spotted both in your hand, in the air, and on the ground! Don't go overboard here, just a few cookies (less than TEN!!) and MOVE ON. You can come back to this behavior (and you will) often in any case.

Baby Nose Bop

OBJECTIVE

You want to teach your puppy that open hands are GOOD things, and encourage her to move toward an open hand in anticipation of a treat appearing in it. You want a nice clean touch of that wet little nose to the palm of your hand, whether your palm is facing up, or down, whether your hand is at your side or outstretched, and whether it is low, or high. You also want to practice good clean delivery of my treats - you will strive to make the treat appear in that open palm, having been delivered from your other hand which was holding the treat in the first place.

This is a training activity for both your puppy and for you! Well, they all are, really, right?

What to do

- Holding some food in one closed fist, present your open palm to your puppy, within easy reach. It's ok to prime the pump and have that open hand smell like food. Present with some flair - use the element of surprise and novelty to get your puppy to focus on the appearance of the hand and investigate it.
- When your puppy bumps into, noses, licks, or otherwise physically interacts with your hand (barring BITING it), quickly place a cookie between your open palm and your puppy's nose/face. If your palm is facing up, you can drop the cookie in it, but try to deliver it such that it goes from placing it on your palm straight in to your puppy's mouth.
- While your puppy is eating the treat, remove both hands, and repeat.

Tips to remember

Make sure you're using food your puppy wants to eat, AND make sure the food is easily spotted both in your hand, and easy for YOU to deliver! Don't go overboard here, just a few cookies (less than TEN!!) and MOVE ON. You can come back to this behavior (and you will) often in any case. I am using kibble for this game, as per my usual.

Voluntary Restrain Or Collar Grab

OBJECTIVE

When you present your open hand, your puppy offers his collar/harness to be held. Your puppy desires to be restrained, as it predicts the beginning of something fun! This activity will later be useful for lots of different games. Also, it helps your puppy to be comfortable with her leash being put on. Being able to grab your puppy without her getting scared can be a lifesaver in a potentially dangerous situation, so this game is very important.

What to do

- Put your hand on your dog's collar/harness/neck and give him a cookie. Make sure to leave your hand on the collar while you reward. Remove your hand after your dog has finished eating.
- Spent a few sessions on this exercise in different environments. It is a classical conditioning exercise. Your dog has to do nothing except tolerate the restraint and eat cookies.

- As your dog learns to expect the cookie, gently tug on the collar/harness or even his fur. Your dog will learn that it is a good thing when you grab him and there is pressure on the collar.
- After a few sessions, present your open hand right next to the collar. Reward if your dog moves towards your hand to be restrained.
- Slowly increase the distance between your dog and your open hand. Now it becomes your puppy's choice to be restrained. If your puppy does not offer to move towards your hand, increase the distance and spent more repetitions on restrain and reward.

Tips to remember

Restrain before you release to a toy, a food machine, or a game of chase with you or other puppies.

Generalize and proof the behavior: Does your puppy offer to be restrained while you sit on the floor? On a chair? While you stand? While you lean over/towards him?

Does your puppy offer to be restrained around agility equipment? When you hold a toy? After you threw a toy?

How to cue

Do not use a verbal cue for this game. If you present my open hand, expect your puppy to come and offer his collar/harness for your to hold. However, you can certainly put a verbal cue on this behavior if you like.

Put On Your Collar

OBJECTIVE

This game is especially important for the sensitive puppy who does not like to have something put over his head. The idea is to play a fun shaping game with your puppy, while working on a life skill. This game will get your puppy used to putting his head through something, which will later be useful for different situations.

Just think about putting a harness, coat or cone on your puppy. It will be very helpful if your puppy does not hate you for putting something over his head!

What to do

- Use a collar that you can make quite a bit bigger than your puppy's head. Have some treats ready. Hold the collar at the bottom with one hand, so that it stands up in a way that your hand is below your puppy's head should she stick it through.
- Mark and reward any interaction with the collar: sniffing, moving towards it, anything.

- Feed your treats through the collar, so that your puppy has to stick his nose through just a bit. After he takes the treat from you, it is okay if he pulls back.
- Now wait for more and more motion directed through the collar. Your puppy will soon stick his nose through the middle, because that is where he expects his treats (rightly so).
- Slowly raise the criteria. Wait for your puppy to stick his head through further and further before you reward, until your puppy puts his head through all the way and thus puts on his collar himself.

Tips to remember

Holding the hand below your puppy's head makes it less threatening for your puppy. It is more difficult if your puppy has to stick his head under your hand that is holding the collar.

Make sure not to lure your puppy's head through the collar, but let him take the initiative and just reward any poke through the hole.

If you have a puppy that is sensitive to having put something over his head, take lots of time for this game. Reward small interactions with the collar at first. Keep the sessions very short. Never lure him, always let him take the initiative. If you lure his head through and he suddenly finds himself with a collar on, he might panic and avoid the collar completely the next time.

Until your puppy is proficient with this game, try to keep the collar on most of the time, unless you are prepared to take the time to play this game. Don't force the collar on your puppy because you are short in time. Rather, leave the collar on.

How to cue

This is a life skill and no verbal cue should be required. Presenting the collar in your hand is a strong enough visual cue for your puppy to understand what you expect him to do.

Running Is FUN

OBJECTIVE

When you run, your puppy should be running after you and come to the side that you are indicating by looking over your respective shoulder. Your puppy should have a desire to chase after you, as soon as you start moving. This is a great game to increase toy drive as well as a desire for running. I play it regularly with all my puppies.

What to do

- Get someone to restrain your puppy for you. Start out just a few feet away from your puppy, holding his favorite toy. Get your puppy's attention and create excitement by making sounds and moving around. When your puppy is focused on you, start running. Once your puppy shows any indication of wanting to follow you, the person restraining him should let go. When your puppy has caught up, start an exciting game of tug.

PERFORMANCE PUPPY ABCs

- Once your puppy understands the game, start using a verbal cue to build excitement. Something like "reeeeady, steeeeady". On the word "go!", your helper should release the puppy and you should start running.
- Be sure to play this game with your puppy on both and your left and on your right. You should hold the toy in the hand where your puppy is. If you look over your left shoulder, your puppy should come to your left side and you should have the toy in your left hand.
- Repeat this game in different environments and with different people restraining your puppy. Vary the distance between you and your puppy before you start running.
- Test if your puppy understands your verbal excitement cue by saying it before you get ready to run off. Does your puppy start pulling forward on the verbal alone?

Tips to remember

For this game, I prefer toys on a long lead. I fold up the toy and let go as I run away, so that the toy is dragging behind me when my dog is running after me. You can also attach a leash to your puppy's favorite toy.

How to cue

Get ready to run and maybe already take a few little steps or jumps as your physical cue. Say "reeeady, steeeady" in an excited tone of voice as a verbal cue. Right before your puppy has caught the toy, you can say "get it".

Beginning With Boxes

OBJECTIVE

You will want to encourage your puppy to be adventuresome when presented with something novel. You will also want your puppy to be able to deal with awkwardness with ease. It's awkward trying to climb in a box when you're not sure how many legs you have! You can move on from this beginning step by making the box smaller, switching to a food bowl, or a tippy board, or whatever you like, but for now, even looking at the box is worth rewarding - and the reward will be delivered to further encourage exploration of the object (ie in the box).

What to do

- Clear the floor of other distractions as best you can, and hold on to your box. Be READY, the first reaction you get will start the ball rolling for your puppy.
- Drop the box, and when your puppy turns toward it, looks at it, sniffs it, ANY reaction, praise and reward by dropping the cookie IN the box in a way that your puppy can see (remember Follow the Food?)

- Feel free to toss more cookies in the box, particularly if your puppy then puts a foot or two in the box. Rectangular boxes are good for this, as you can put a cookie on a far end, encouraging a step inside by your puppy to get to it. Extra praise for rear legs in the box!
- Have your puppy follow some food in your hand to get her OUT of the box, pick up the box, and then repeat.

Tips to remember

Make sure you're using food your puppy wants to eat, AND make sure the food is easily spotted when you toss it in the box. Don't go overboard here, just a few cookies (less than TEN!!) and MOVE ON. You can come back to this behavior as often as you like - it's a good game to revisit, just for fun!

Beginning Red Light, Green Light

OBJECTIVE

In the short term, you want your puppy to learn not to maul your hands. Ouch! Those teeth! As far as the big picture goes, you'd like your puppy to learn that there are behaviors other than mauling you hand that will 'unlock' the food you hold in it. You don't really need to worry about WHAT your puppy does - ultimately your puppy might offer any one of several behaviors when it sees you have a closed hand of food. You want your puppy to learn that any behavior other than mauling your hand will get you to open that hand and feed your puppy from it.

What to do

- Let your puppy see you put some food in your hand. Don't put too much food in your hand at once - you don't want it to go flying everywhere when you open your hand. Just 2-3 treats, or even ONE, is fine.
- Present your closed fist to your puppy's nose. As soon as your puppy backs off even a millimeter, open your hand just a bit. Of course, usually this action will send your puppy back in to mauling your hands, so be prepared to CLOSE your hand immediately

PERFORMANCE PUPPY ABCs

- Continue in this vein until your puppy STAYS back off of your hand long enough for you to reach in with your other hand to deliver a treat, OR until you can then give your puppy the food out of your now open hand
- Repeat! You may be at steps 1-2 for a while, don't be in a rush. You can also give your puppy treats out of your OTHER hand if you need to diminish your puppy's focus on your closed hand.

Tips to remember

Don't put so much food in your hand that it can fall out of or be knocked out of your hand easily. If your puppy decides to back up and/or sit, that's just fine! You just want your puppy to explore her options with and to NOT maul your hand, and right now, your puppy doesn't need to narrow it down any further than that!

Beginning Red Light, Green Light - Food Bowl Manners

OBJECTIVE

You want your puppy to offer a sit when it sees you with a bowl of food in your hands, ready to put the bowl down on the floor. You want your puppy to REMAIN seated until the bowl is on the ground, and your hands are off of it, and you say your release word "OK".

What to do

- Put a few kibble in a bowl and hold the bowl above your puppy's eye level. When your puppy offers a sit, lower the bowl just a bit. When your puppy breaks its sit, lift the bowl back up, and start to lower again when your puppy sits.
- If your puppy remains seated as the bowl comes down, remove a piece of food from the bowl and give it to your puppy directly. You can continue to lower the bowl while your puppy is eating, or while you're feeding your puppy, so long as your puppy remains seated. If at any time

the sit is broken, lift the bowl back up. As your puppy gets more patient with the sit, this can be omitted.

- Continue lowering the bowl to the floor as long as your puppy remains seated. Raise it any time your puppy leans forward or lifts its rear, and lower it when your puppy is sitting again.
- Progress toward tapping the bowl on the floor, setting the bowl on the floor but keeping hands on it, then putting the bowl on the floor, removing hands, and saying "OK". Not all in one session, of course!

Tips to remember

You're working with a puppy that wants to MOVE and has a short attention span. Don't ask for too much duration too soon, and don't ask for too many repetitions of this. I just put a few kibble in a bowl while the grown up dogs are having their breakfast or dinner, and do this 2-3 times together with my puppy. This exercise also affords your puppy the opportunity to see that you taking the bowl away is not the END of the food, so there's no reason to get upset when you remove the bowl; it's just an opportunity to play the game again! Aside from meals, this can be done as a short, fun training session with just a few kibble placed in the bowl each time. Keep it short, keep it fun, don't make your puppy be still for too long!

Laying On Your Side

OBJECTIVE

If you ever had a dog who has had treatments by a massage or physical therapist, you know the importance of having a dog who will relax when being treated by a stranger. It is not a natural behavior for dogs to lay on their side and expose themselves, unless they feel like they are in a safe environment. For this reason, it is important to teach your puppy to lay on his side when asked. Mastering this trick will make treatments more effective, as your puppy is more relaxed. Additionally, it will help you with grooming you puppy.

What to do

- Have a few pieces of kibble ready. Ask your puppy to lie down and reward him. Use a piece of kibble to lure your puppy's nose over his shoulder, so that he flops over. Reward.

- If your puppy doesn't flop on his side yet, reward every inclination towards flopping over (weight shifting, rear end flopping on the side, etc.). Increase the flopping a little more with each repetition.
- Once your puppy is comfortable with the action of flopping over, increase the duration that you expect your puppy to stay on his side. For this, feed him several pieces of food one after the other while he is laying on his side.
- Increase the intervals in which you reward your puppy.
- Start touching and manipulating your puppy while he is laying on his side. Reward if he can tolerate it and stays.
- Ask friends to touch your puppy while he is laying on his side, so that he gets used to other people touching him.

Tips to remember

When flopping over on their side, puppies expose their underside, which is often uncomfortable to them, as they feel unprotected. For this reason it is important to start this trick in a safe and comfortable environment without strange people or dogs around. Once your puppy gains more confidence in this exercise, you can ask for the behavior in more crowded environments. Always work both sides.

How to cue

I use a hand lure to flip your puppy over. I also use the verbal cue "sleep".

Accepting Boundaries

OBJECTIVE

Wouldn't it be nice not having a baby gate at every doorway you don't want your dog to go through? Teaching your puppy to accept boundaries allows for just that. An automatic wait at certain doorways or gates is a very useful life skill to have. It can also be a lifesaver, when a door or gate is left open by accident. Further, waiting before bolting through a gate keeps your puppy from crashing into other dogs or being pushed or run over when multiple excited dogs are trying to fit through a doorway all at once.

What to do

- Find a door or gate at which you would like your puppy to wait and ask permission before going through (front door, garage door, gate to property, ...)
- Put your puppy on a leash and have some kibble ready to reward her. Go through the gate and leave your puppy on the other side. Your puppy will likely try to follow you. Every

time your puppy makes an attempt to move through the gate, push it closed so that your puppy cannot fit through.

- When you see any sign of retreat (puppy sitting down, moving backwards a step or just shifting her weight back), open the gate a bit and reward her as long as she is not showing any forward motion. If she attempts to go through the gate, you close it.
- It may take several repetitions until you can actually reward your puppy for not making an attempt to follow you. That is okay.
- Make sure to close the gate as soon as there is any forward motion from your puppy. In the first session you might be busy opening and closing the gate quite a lot and not get many repetitions in.
- With every session your puppy will remember sooner to shift back and wait to get rewarded. You can now start to release your puppy through the gate after you have rewarded her choice of staying.
- Once your puppy is pretty confident with the boundary, you can open the gate, move through and leave the gate open. Move away one step and go back immediately to reward. Slowly build up distance and duration.
- Once your puppy has a good automatic wait, add distractions (drop a toy or kibble behind the boundary, say random words but not the release word, call other dogs through while your puppy has to wait, be creative). This will test your puppy's concentration and further your puppy's understanding.

Tips to remember

There may be several repetitions where you cannot reward, as your puppy is moving towards you too soon. That is okay. Remember, your action of opening the gate even a little bit is a reward in itself.

Once you decide to establish this boundary at a certain gateway, make sure to not let your puppy pass without prior permission. If you are short on time, carry your puppy across if you need to.

In this exercise, never tell your puppy to stay or wait. You want it to be her decision. Only this will allow you to trust her to accept the boundary later even when you are not around to reinforce the wait.

This is a great exercise to transfer to crates or car doors, so that your puppy doesn't bolt out.

How to cue

As you want an automatic wait, never say any cue for your puppy to stay. When you release your puppy through the gate, say her name. You can use a general release word such as OK if all dogs can safely pass through the gate at the same time.

The Dog Door

OBJECTIVE

Teach your puppy to go in and out of a double flap dog door on her own. This, along with a strong association with going potty in the designated area on the exterior side of this dog door, will lead to her being able to let herself out to go to the bathroom. You may not be able to trust her to let herself out for quite some time, BUT, you can start asking her to use the dog door when you TAKE her out to go to the bathroom, to create a routine.

What to do

- Lift the flap/s, and encourage your puppy to come near to, or put a foot on or in the dog door floor or the flap. She can nose the flap, paw at the flap, put a foot on the floor of the dog door, etc. Hold both flaps up and stick your cookie-laden hand through, luring her, and drop a handful of treats on the other side, so the flap closes behind her.
- Lift the flaps and call your puppy back through. This goes a bit faster with two people, calling back and forth.
- Gradually let the flaps fall on your puppy as she goes through.
- Hold treats near to the flap and reward your puppy for pushing on the flap with her paws. Deliver the reward toward the center of the dog door, between the two flaps, and then

further lure her through and drop more cookies on the ground on the other side of the dog door.

- Repeat a few times, then move on to something else!

Tips to remember

Make sure you have several treats in hand for each go-round of this behavior. You'll want treats to lure your puppy through the dog door AND treats to scatter on the ground on the other SIDE of the dog door. Because I'm dishing out so many treats, I have to be careful how long I do this - it'll end up being most of a meal!

Chase The Handler

OBJECTIVE

We will build on the previous game of "running is fun". However, in this game, nobody is restraining your puppy. Instead we wait for your puppy to lose focus and then encourage him to chase us.

This game will increase your puppy's focus on you, even when you are not actively working with him. It will also help with toy drive and motivation.

It is a great game to transition your puppy from sniffing time to working time in a class or seminar setting. While listening to the instructor your puppy may sniff. When it is time to run again, you can use this game to get him excited and focused and move him to the start line.

If you have a grown dog that is likely to be distracted at shows, this game will help you to get him back in the game.

What to do

- Have a toy that your dog likes in your pocket. Wander around and wait for your puppy to lose focus and start sniffing. Get a few feet away from your puppy, say "reeeady" and start running. If your puppy is chasing you, great! As soon as he catches up, bring out the toy and play. If your puppy is not interested in you running away, make sure that:
    - you are very close to your puppy when you run away, making exciting sounds
    - your puppy sufficiently understands the previous game "Running is Fun" and gets excited when you say "ready"
    - whatever your puppy is interested in at the moment is not more interesting than you (i.e. make sure your puppy is not finding meatballs on the ground while you are running away)
- Try to get a head start by wandering on the opposite side of an obstacle, so you can play catch with your puppy around it. Soccer goals work great for this purpose.
- Play this game in different environments. When putting agility equipment away, leave out the tunnels and play a game of chase around them.
- When your puppy really understands this game, try to carefully increase the distraction.

Tips to remember

It is best to play this game in a field with some natural "obstacles" in it, so that you can run around them and get a head start. For puppies that don't know agility equipment yet, you can play this game on an agility course and use tunnels or jumps as obstacles. Please be safe and make sure your puppy can't accidentally get on a contact and fall off.

The most important part in this game is for you to actually feel the adrenalin kick in as you run from your puppy! This game should be a rush for both of you to play, because excitement is contagious! For this game, I prefer toys on a long lead. I fold up the toy and let go as I run away, so that the toy is dragging behind me when my puppy is running after me. You can also attach a leash to your puppy's favorite toy.

How to cue

The only thing I say in this game is "ready" before I start running.

Recalls From Food/Toys

OBJECTIVE

By now you have most likely discovered that your puppy has a preference for toys over food or vice versa. Either preference is fine and nothing to worry about. However, for future training it is helpful if your puppy finds both toys and food rewarding. For this reason food is used for some games, while toys are used for others. In order to help your puppy learn to switch between food and toys, it is useful to first teach her to call off of either and take the other as a reward. This skill is also important when working with external reinforcements later on in training. If your puppy steals the toy/food that you have placed, it will make training more difficult. Further, this game will strengthen your puppy's recalls.

What to do

- Think about the preferences of your puppy. Does she like food or toys better? You should have a reward that your puppy prefers, and a helper should have a less favored reward.
- Ask the helper to feed/play with your puppy for a bit. Then ask your puppy to stop and become passive. Once you see a decent chance of your puppy responding, call her and reward with the preferred reward.
- Call your puppy a little sooner with each repetition, until your helper is not becoming passive anymore, but still actively involved with your puppy, and your puppy still comes when you call.
- Now switch rewards and repeat. If your puppy prefers food, give your helper some boring food to start with. If your puppy prefers toys, equip your helper with a boring toy and give instructions to not play too animatedly in the beginning.
- If your puppy is still successful with the recall, you have done a very good job teaching it! You can further increase the challenge by making the helper''s reward better (higher value treats or engaging play time).

Tips to remember

Full mastery of this game is very difficult for young puppies. If you cannot call your puppy off a helper when that helper is actively engaging with your puppy, instruct your helper to become passive and reward your puppy for coming at that point. Check back on the status of this exercise after a couple months. As the bond between you and your puppy strengthens, this exercise should become easier.

Make sure to be more interesting than your helper. You can make exciting sounds or squeak a toy in order to encourage your puppy to call off the helper.

How to cue

Make sure to only use your recall cue when it seems likely that your puppy will respond. If she is still licking your helper's hands for treats, wait for her to stop and then call.

Recalls With Distractions

OBJECTIVE

This game teaches your puppy to come straight to you when she hears her name – no matter how many interesting things she has to pass by on her way. Your puppy will learn that it always pays to come to you, even if there are other interesting things around.

This is a great foundation for any future performance dog. There are plenty of good smells, tasty treats and fun toys at shows, however we would like our dogs to ignore those and focus on us and our performance.

What to do

- Take a moment to reflect on how strong your puppy's recalls are. Be honest: Have been spending enough cookies on your puppy coming to you? Is your puppy mostly confident and excited when you call her name and rushes back to you? If that is not the case yet, spend more time on basic recalls before proceeding with this upgrade.

- If you deem your puppy ready for a challenge, get some treats and her food bowl. Send your puppy to her mat and have her stay (alternatively a helper can hold her). Place the EMPTY food bowl several yards away to your puppy's left and position yourself to your puppy's right. The empty bowl, your puppy and you should form a triangle. Call your puppy to you and reward heavily if she comes straight to you without checking out the bowl. If your puppy darts to the bowl instead, calmly walk over, put your hand in her collar and move her past the bowl. Release her when she is not interested in the bowl anymore, call her name and reward.

- If your puppy is not choosing you over the bowl yet, spend more time on your basic recalls and make sure to always reward very enthusiastically with high value reinforcement. If your puppy came straight to you, you have done a great job so far. Time to built in more distractions.

- First, put a piece of kibble in the bowl so that your puppy sees it. Call your puppy and reward it from hand with a high value reinforcement.

- When your puppy is successful with this exercise, gradually move the food bowl closer to the path that your puppy has to take to get to your position.

- Finally, move the food bowl in your puppy's path. This may seem like an impossible task at first. It can only be mastered if your puppy really understands that the most important reinforcement comes from you, rather than from her environment. This level of distraction requires a certain level of maturity and might be too much for younger puppies. Give your puppy some time and try again after a few weeks if she does not succeed at it yet.

Tips to remember

Is your puppy more interested in food or toys? Choose the least interesting thing for your first distraction (i.e. replace the food bowl with a toy, if your puppy is really into food). Then work your way up to distractions that are of higher value to your puppy.

Check your top ten rewards list. You might even discover that your puppy's priorities have changed since you created that list.

How to cue

Call your puppy by name or by your recall cue, whichever you prefer.

Beginning Balance Board

OBJECTIVE

The objective here is ONLY to have a little fun with your puppy on an unstable surface. This is NOT about conditioning or strength training or anything like that; your puppy is too young for that sort of thing in my mind. I want her to be comfortable getting on AND to know how to get OFF of it as well, so that she doesn't feel she is trapped without escape.

Wobble boards, tippy boards, or balance boards are all the same thing, just called by different names.

What to do

- Use any tippy surface - a board with a ball underneath, an inflated pillow, a wobble board. Improvise and remember that your puppy does not care how much money you spent on this, so, the less the better.

- Lure your puppy up and on to the wobble board. Take your time. One foot is better than none, and it may be that you need to first reward your dog for taking interest visually, then moving near to, then touching, then climbing on the tippy board.
- Almost as soon as you CAN lure your puppy up and on to the balance board, either lure your puppy OFF or toss some treats off in a way that your puppy notices. For many puppies, luring them OFF before they're finished looking for cookies you may have sprinkled on the tippy board will make them turn right around and try to get back on.

Tips to remember

This activity is just for exposure and fun. There's no goal other than that. Time spent on this activity should be kept short (ten cookies or less!). Your puppy doesn't need a formal conditioning program, she's far too young for that. She just needs to flop around and get comfortable in awkward situations, and learn to laugh it off. Have fun, keep it short, and don't try to keep your puppy ON the tippy board. Remember that preventing access can increase desire - so if you really want your puppy to want to be ON that board, sprinkle some treats on it, pick her up, and set her down a few feet away, and see if she doesn't head right TO the board!

Navigating Nature's Obstacles

OBJECTIVE

For her future performance career, your puppy will need good body awareness for a variety of exercises and obstacles. A great way to improve your puppy's coordination and balancing skills is to use "obstacles" that you find in your environment. It is an added bonus that walks with your puppy will become very interesting for both of you. If your puppy thinks that you are the coolest person to make up all kinds of fun games on walks, she will be less likely to engage in unwanted behavior such as looking for animals to chase or yucky things to eat and roll in.

What to do

- Find an obstacle, such as a fallen tree, a low wall, a tree stump, a rock or similar. Be creative!
- Ask your puppy to climb on it. The first few times you may lure her, but try to fade the lure quickly. Make it a shaping game, waiting for your puppy to offer to interact with the obstacle.
- Don't LURE your puppy over balancing obstacles. Rather, if she slows down, let her figure it out herself, rewarding every little step she takes. It is okay if she wants to jump down. Give her time to discover the obstacle in her pace.

Tips to remember

Play this game with as many different obstacles as you can think of. It is great exposure to new situations and will create confidence in your puppy once she masters the obstacles. Remember to make sure your obstacles are safe, so that your puppy can't hurt herself falling off. There are no rules as to how to perform the obstacles. Just go with what your puppy offers. The main idea is for her to interact with them while at the same time working on coordination skills.

How to cue

I don't use a formal cue for this game, just my general 'action'. This cue tells your puppy to try out behaviors. I use it whenever I start a shaping session.

PERFORMANCE PUPPY ABCs

Beginning Manners Minder

OBJECTIVE

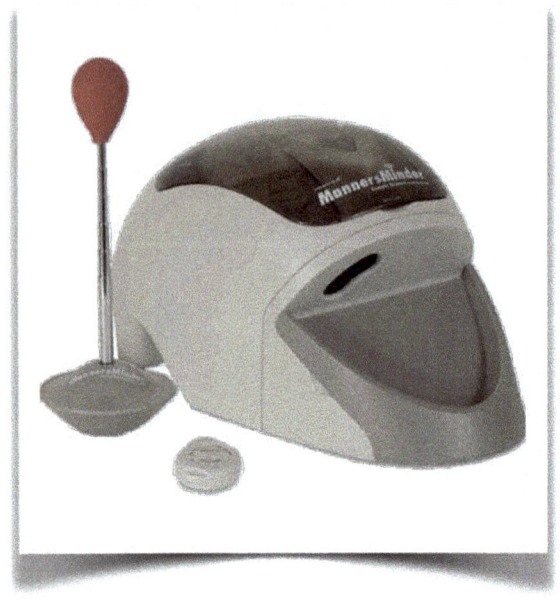

The Manners Minder is a tool that I use extensively in my agility training with my dogs. For now, I just want you to introduce it to your puppy, and teach her that the beep and the dispensing of food from the Manners Minder is a consequence of some action, ANY action, on her part. At first, you may just let her eat from the tray without asking too much of her, but, depending on her confidence with the whirring and beeping of the machine, you can move toward asking for specific behaviors to get a treat. You don't really need to have any behaviors in mind here; you just want her to learn that any behavior other than staring, praying, or scratching at the Manners Minder is likely to earn a treat. Then, move on from there!

What to do

- Fill the Manners Minder with a treat it will dispense. Just use your puppy's kibble
- Set the Manners Minder on the ground, and let your puppy sniff for a bit

- Turn the Manners Minder on and press the button on the remote to dispense some treats
- As your puppy's curiosity and confidence dictate, move on toward very simple behaviors that she already has familiarity with, so she learns that treats come from the MM as well as from the hand.

Tips to remember

Make sure you start with a hungry puppy! Don't push your puppy too quickly to get comfortable with the MM. You're not going to be using the Manners Minder formally for months and months yet, so right now, it's all about moving at your puppy's pace, comfort, and FUN. Sometimes it helps to let a timid puppy see other dogs getting excited about the MM. Even if your puppy is watching from the comfort of a nearby crate, she'll be watching and soaking it all in.

Beginning Rear Foot Targeting

OBJECTIVE

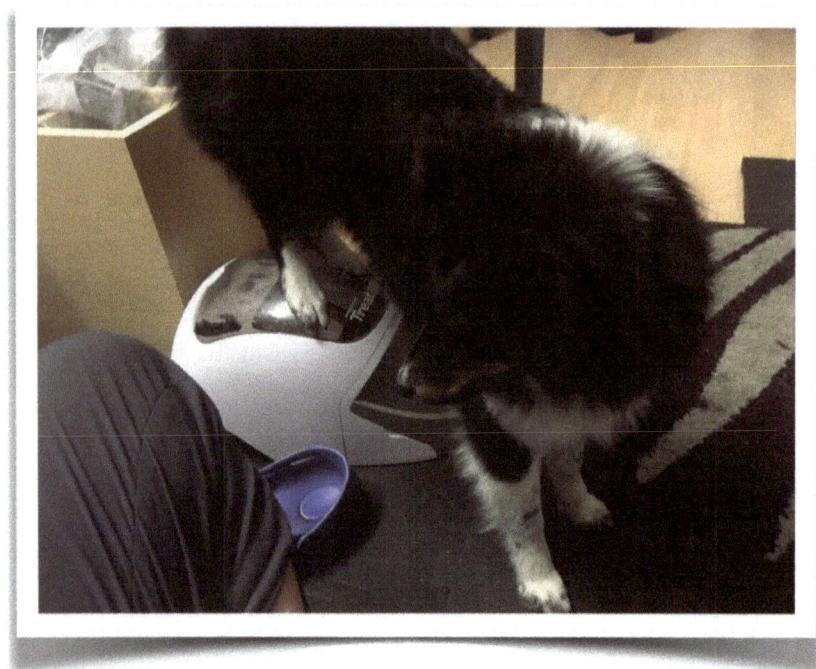

As with most of the things you're working on at the moment, this is just an introduction for your puppy. It's an introduction to the concept that she can get rewarded for things having to do with her rear feet; having them on a different surface than her front feet, moving them in response to a cue (you touching them, etc.), picking them up, etc. Of course dogs are aware of their rear feet, BUT, what they're NOT aware of, typically, is that doing things WITH their rear feet will earn reinforcement.

There's no need to have your puppy backing up just YET, although that will come soon after this. At first, you just want her to get comfortable being on two different surfaces for a reward. Most dogs don't like backing up on to an object at first, as they don't like to bang their hocks on things they can't see. So when you DO tackle that behavior, you should start with something soft. But for now…

What to do

- Start with a low object that is stable and has a texture different than that of the floor upon which it rests. I just used a piece of shelving that was handy. You can use a pillow or other small soft object as well.
- Lure your puppy across the object and stop her when her back feet are on the object. Click and let her eat the food she has been following.
- Raise the object up a bit for more contrast with the floor - I leaned my shelving on the baseboard of the nearby wall.
- ALSO: hold some cookies in your hand, and arrange things such that you can reach your puppy's back legs. As you reach for a back leg, open your hand and let your puppy eat the food. Touch, or hold and lift the back leg as your puppy allows, but just for a moment. When you let go of the leg or take your hand off of it, close your food hand. You can use a target stick for this if you can't reach; it can be a bit awkward.

Tips to remember

This is a very rudimentary introduction to having the back feet on a different surface than the front feet, AND to you handling your puppy's rear feet. There's no need to rush things here, just get your puppy familiar with the idea that this is yet ANOTHER weird thing you're going to do with them. In the next few days to come, we will expand on this behavior in a variety of directions, some of which may or may not include the use of the Manners Minder.

The Two Toy Game - Get The Live Toy

OBJECTIVE

This fun game will not only teach your puppy how to play with a toy of my choosing, but it will also help her learn how to redirect from one toy to another, and can serve as the beginning of a verbal release of a toy. This game will also serve as the first step to teaching a retrieve to your puppy. For this game, you will have two identical toys. Your objective is to get your puppy tugging on one of the toys actively, and then, when it goes "dead" and the toy in your other hand goes "live", your puppy will come off the dead toy and on to the live toy.

What to do

- First, I'll need several identical toys. I like the toys shown above; they're inexpensive to make and puppies seem to like the fringe. I'm by no means the inventor of this type of toy - this idea has been around longer than I've been in dog training! Get some large diameter rope at the hardware store, and a roll of duct tape. Cut the rope into sections, wrap the tape around the middle of each section, and then pull the rope apart on the ends to make a fringe.

- IF YOUR PUPPY DOES NOT LIKE TO TUG: While you can take the time to clicker train a puppy to tug, and I've done it, it's easier and more fun to simply find a toy that your puppy WILL tug with. Be creative! If you've got a food motivated puppy, then it's time to put something truly stinky and NASTY in a sock, and start waving that sock around!
- To start the game, I'll get your puppy tugging on one toy, with the other toy hidden underneath me as I'm sitting on the ground. After a short while, I will pin the "live" toy (the one she's tugging on) down to the ground, STILL HOLDING ON TO IT, and let it be "dead". At the same time, I will produce the second toy, and make a production of wiggling it around so that it attracts your puppy's attention. I WILL NOT MOVE THIS TOY TOWARD Your puppy IN ANY WAY, SHAPE, OR FORM! It's important that your puppy come TO the toy. I never wave a toy in your puppy's face, if I'm employing good practices.
- When your puppy moves from the live toy to the dead toy, I will keep the dead toy out, and dead, pinned under my hand. After a few moments of lively tugging on the live toy with your puppy, I will pin THAT toy to the ground, making it the dead toy, and will instantly bring the OTHER toy to life.
- I will then repeat the game a few times, always making sure to set up the live toy so that your puppy comes TO the toy, rather than the toy to your puppy.
- If I find that your puppy is coming off the live toy in anticipation of the dead toy becoming live, I will leave the dead toy dead, and keep the live toy active, so that your puppy's attention is drawn back to it!
- After a short while (less than 2-3 minutes), the game is over, until the next time!

Tips to remember

Keep the game short, and fun! Tugging enthusiastically is a lot of fun but expends a lot of energy and requires a lot of focus; a minute is plenty of time to spend on this game. Make sure your puppy wants to pull on your tug toy - this means that you may need to put a hot dog or some liver pate in a sock (or a chicken neck, if you feed raw), or get creative in some other way, but the chances are good there IS something that YOUR puppy considers worth pulling on with his or her mouth!

You can start saying things like "get it" as a toy becomes live. In this way, your puppy will start to associate a verbal cue with going toward a toy. You won't really NEED to work on a verbal release at this time, because your puppy is learning that there is incentive to release off a dead toy and to a live one, and so a verbal release later will be simpler to teach, because you've already captured the behavior of letting go of a toy, and you'll simply need to mark and reward it as you see fit!

The Two Toy Game - Beginning Retrieve

OBJECTIVE

You're going to build off of GET THE LIVE TOY, and COLLAR GRAB exercises with this game, and create a situation where your puppy will pick up a toy that has been tossed a short distance away, and bring it back to me, to play with a toy you have on your person. Keep things short and sweet in the beginning, and don't have any expectations beyond retrieving just a few feet. You'll build off of this behavior with respect to distance, as well as your own motion away from your puppy.

What to do

- You'll need 2-3 of my homemade identical frizzy toys on hand. Sit on the floor, with the extra toys hidden underneath or behind you.

- While playing GET THE LIVE TOY, on the floor with your puppy, wait for a moment while your puppy is readjusting the toy in her mouth, or has temporarily lost her grip on it. Then simultaneously grab your puppy's collar with one hand, while you move the live toy out of reach.
- Hold your puppy back by the collar while you quickly and animatedly toss the toy just a foot or two out of reach, and then INSTANTLY let go of your puppy as she shows interest in going toward the toy. You might say "get it" while you do this, as part of the excited noises you're making, since that's what you'll eventually say to her to get a toy you've tossed or would like her to retrieve.
- The moment your puppy latches on to the toy she has, it's considered "dead", and you will have a second toy out, in hand, whipping it around on the floor, while you continue making animated noises, including her name (if you know she will respond to it). The first toy, being frizzy, gets stuck in her teeth pretty easily, which is a GOOD thing, because she almost can't help but bring it back as she hears me making noise with the new "live toy".
- As your puppy comes back to your hand with the live toy to tug, reach for the dead toy to bring it back underneath or behind you, and then you can repeat the game.

Tips to remember

If you're unsure about your puppy's ability to come back to the new live toy in your hand, you may want to go back and work more on GET THE LIVE TOY before working on this game. Also, if you think your puppy may want to run toward me and then past me to get away and play with the toy herself, you can position yourself with your back toward the entryway of a small room, so you can predict the direction your puppy is going to run with the toy and be there to grab it as she runs past, and continue the game.

PERFORMANCE PUPPY ABCs

You should also have played enough of the BEGINNING NAME RECOGNITION game that your puppy knows what to do when she hears you screeching just after she's run away - run back toward you! You may need to play that game a few more times with food, as a reminder, before attempting this part of the two toy game.

Keep your sessions short with respect to distance and duration - you want the toy you tossed to remain within arm's reach, if your puppy doesn't bring it back and instead just runs back to your new live toy. Also, if you use a toy that is somewhat frizzy and difficult to disengage from, your puppy will be more likely to be able to bring it, maybe by accident at first, but then more and more purposefully. As your puppy is reliably bringing the frizzy toy back, you can switch out to toys that require more purposeful effort to carry back, but don't progress faster than your puppy dictates, and always have multiples of whatever toy you're using, so that you can use identical toys for this game!

The Two Toy Game - Adding Motion To A Retrieve

OBJECTIVE

You will want to build on the two previous steps in the TWO TOY GAME and add some motion to the retrieve, to encourage your puppy to bring the toy back to you even more quickly, and with the added distraction of your motion.

What to do

- Using two identical toys (see previous exercises for the two toy game to see the toys we recommend using), get your puppy tugging on one of the two toys. Make sure that you have the other toy handy, but unavailable to your puppy

- As your puppy is tugging, put your hand in your puppy's collar, align your puppy so that she is pointed away from you, and hold the toy still momentarily.
- When your puppy lets go of the toy, immediately toss it just a few feet in front of your puppy so that she has to move away from you to get the toy. Make sure you don't PUSH your puppy toward the toy - simply let go of the collar when your puppy pulls on it to get to the thrown toy.
- As your puppy reaches the thrown toy, move away animatedly, and bring the other toy in to play as your puppy reaches you. The game is now the DEAD TOY, LIVE TOY game!
- When your puppy is tugging excitedly on the new live toy, repeat the steps above!

Tips to remember

Make sure that the toys you have are toys that your puppy wants to play with. If a rope with tape around it will do, use that. If you need socks filled with liverwurst, use THAT. Whatever your puppy will grab on to and hold on to - use it! If you're using a food sock you MAY want to reserve BETTER treats in the sock you hold on to, at first, so that your puppy doesn't get so engrossed in the food she just got a hold of that she forget s about what she could also be getting from you.

Remember that fuzzy toys, or toys made of soft fabric, may be more likely to "stick" in your puppy's mouth - they will be easier for your puppy to carry, and therefore easier for her to just about **accidentally** bring back to you.

Don't toss the toy any further than you think your puppy can handle - if you start with less than a foot, that's totally fine. Build up slowly, over time. It's better to play this game just a few times (fewer than five!), to develop real enthusiasm for the game, than to repeat it over and over and over, when you could be doing something ELSE fun with your puppy (who can only focus for a couple of minutes anyway!).

Racing To The Toy

OBJECTIVE

Once your puppy chases after a toy that is being pulled away from her, it is time to introduce a toy that is not moving (dead toy). This game aims to increase your puppy's drive to the dead toy. At the same time, your puppy learns to run next to you while focusing ahead, helping to prevent behavior such as snapping at the handler or spinning in front of the handler when later running an agility course.

What to do

- Start with a quick game of tug to get your puppy excited about the toy.
- Ask your puppy to offer to be restrained by holding out your hand. Restrain your puppy with one hand and toss the toy a few feet away with your other hand. Use your "reeeady, steeeady" cue to build up excitement.
- Gently push your puppy back and run to the toy. If you reach the toy first, pick it up and play with it yourself. Don't let your puppy have it, but make sure to play exuberantly

PERFORMANCE PUPPY ABCs

enough for your puppy to WANT the toy. If your puppy reaches the toy first – great! Have an exciting game of tug with her.
- Once your puppy understands the game, increase the distance to the toy. You will have to run more and more to actually beat your puppy after a few repetitions.

Tips to remember

Nobody likes losing all the time. If you won a race, make sure to let your puppy win the next! Winning increases your puppy's confidence and will make her try harder after losing.

Any toy that allows you to tug with your dog is fine. It should be easy for you to grab from the ground, or you will never win a race against your puppy.

If your puppy likes to take off with the toy she won, tie a thin long line to the toy, so that you can prevent your puppy from running off with it.

How to cue

Say "reeeady, steeeady" in an excited tone of voice to built up excitement. Your body language should also represent excitement. Before releasing your puppy to the toy, say your toy cue, something like "get it".

Send To Dead Toy

OBJECTIVE

Now that your puppy is familiar with many different toy games, it is time to work on her drive to a toy that is not moving, a so-called 'dead toy'.

The purpose of this game is to create a desire in your puppy to run to and pick up a toy that is on the ground. Mastering this game will help in various training situations. Placing a dead toy as external reinforcement is commonly used in agility training when working on independent obstacle performance, for example.

Additionally, this game is a first introduction to the concept of independently doing something, while the handler is moving in a different direction and can thus help with independent obstacle performance in your dog's agility education and great sends!

What to do

- Start with a quick game of tug to get your puppy excited about the toy.

- Put your puppy in a waiting position (sit, down, stand or on her mat). Reward her for staying a couple times, then drop the toy a few yards from your puppy. Stand next to the toy. Release your puppy and tell her to get the toy. As soon as she picks it up, you run in the opposite direction (where she was waiting). Once your puppy has caught up, you play a game of tug.
- Start with the same setup (puppy stays, you drop the toy a few yards away), however this time you position yourself slightly closer to your puppy, so that she has to run past you to get the toy. Release your puppy and tell her to get the toy, run in the opposite direction once she gets it and play as a reward.
- Incrementally, move yourself closer to your puppy and further from the toy, until you can send your puppy from a location next to you.
- It is time to add your motion. Move in the opposite direction JUST BEFORE your puppy is about to pick up the toy. Reward once she has caught up.
- With each try, move in the opposite direction a little sooner, until you can release your puppy, tell her to get the toy and immediately run off while she is still on her way to the toy. Once she picks it up and catches up with you, play.

Tips to remember

Add your motion gradually. Moving away too quickly or too suddenly is a difficult stimulus for puppies to overcome. After all, we have spent so much time to teach them to chase after and follow you! Make sure to progress in very small steps and don't let your puppy fail twice. If your puppy follows your motion rather than running to the toy, move a little bit later the next time.

Remember to work both sides. Try to get your puppy turning towards you for both directions. If your puppy turns away from you, stay closer to the toy and try to encourage her to turn "correctly". It is important that your puppy is comfortable turning both ways.

How to cue

OK, "get it"

Use your release word and your verbal for sending to the toy. Position yourself so that your feet are facing towards the toy. You may also use a hand gesture to send your puppy. Make sure to use the same arm as the side your puppy is on.

Flirt Pole Fun

OBJECTIVE

A flirt pole is basically a toy on a string tied to a stick. The purpose of using a flirt pole is for your puppy to get excited about playing with the toy. Using a flirt pole, it is easy to move the toy very quickly and in an exciting way, without having to be faster than your puppy constantly. After all, fast quick movements are the movements of prey, so your puppy naturally is interested in anything that moves in such a way.

Later, this game can be used to test impulse control.

What to do

- If you don't want to buy a flirt pole (a cat toy will do for small puppies), you can build one yourself. Use a toy that is easy for you puppy to grab and tug on and tie a light leash to it. Tie the other end of the leash to a broomstick or jump bar.
- Have a helper hold your puppy while you wiggle the toy end of the flirt pole on the ground a few feet away from your puppy. Once you have generated some interested in your puppy for the toy, the helper should release her. Draw the toy away, but let her catch it pretty quickly, then let her tug or run loops with it.

- Take the toy from your puppy and repeat. With each repetition, increase the duration for which your puppy has to chase the toy before letting her catch it. If your puppy looses interest, make sure she catches the toy quickly in the next repetition and then give her a break.
- Once your puppy is familiar with the game, you don't need a helper to start it. You can either restrain your puppy yourself (this requires some coordination with the pole and your puppy), or start her in a control position such as sit, down, stand or on the mat.

Tips to remember

Keep the number of repetitions very low. This is an exciting, but exhausting game. Give your puppy a break after about three tries.

If your puppy is not interested in your flirt pole, try different toys. Maybe she would prefer something squeaky, something soft, or something fluffy and pink. Seriously, Take's favorite toy is a fluffy pink flirt pole for cats - so be creative.

How to cue

Other than your "reeeady, steeeady" and "get it" cue for the toy, there is no cue required in this game. Just have a few crazy minutes playing with your puppy.

1 Minute Motivation

OBJECTIVE

In almost every puppy's training there comes a time when your puppy is distracted and not very motivated to do things with you. For those cases it is good to have a backup plan in the back of your head. If you find your puppy unable to focus, switch from your initial training plan to this game. It might be all you will do in that session, depending on how your puppy is holding up - and that is okay! After all, the most important thing in any training session is not the progress you make on a behavior, but for you and your puppy to enjoy yourselves. Even if it is just for one minute.

What to do

- Think about all the toy games that were introduced so far. Which ones did you and your puppy enjoy the most? Games with one toy or two toys? Games where she would chase you or chase the toy? Games in which you raced her or in which you send her to the toy? Pick two or three favorites, which you will be playing in this session.
- Equip yourself with suitable toys for the games you chose. Make a plan in your head which game to play first, second, and if you have time, third.
- Set a timer to one minute and start the first game, followed by the second and possibly third.
- When you hear the timer go off, finish the game you are playing and then end the session. Give your puppy a break for at least several hours before going back to your initial training goal or playing this game again.

Tips to remember

Consider possible reasons why your puppy is unable to focus in the first place. Is it too hot? Is your puppy tired? Has she had opportunity to go to the bathroom? Is she teething? Are there new distractions that she is not used to (other dogs or people around, for example)? Is she afraid of something?

There are many more possible reasons for a puppy to loose concentration. Sometimes it is difficult to even pinpoint the exact reason. Don't stress about it! Most likely it is a developmental stage that will pass quickly. Just enjoy one minute of fun time and then leave your puppy be.

Don't cheat on the time! One minute is plenty of time if you need to be making sure your puppy is 100% focused on the game. Make your games so exciting and keep the pace so quick, that your puppy has no time to get distracted.

There may be periods in your puppy's development in which this game is all I play, as her brain is under construction and not ready to process other information anyway.

How to cue

No cues needed. Have fun and be crazy!

Come To My Side

OBJECTIVE

From the first day your new puppy moves in with you, make sure it is rewarded A LOT! Many of the rewards are given to your puppy when it is in front of you. This is only natural to us humans, as we interact with others face to face. However, when thinking about your puppy's future in any performance sport, the instances when you want your puppy to be facing you are limited. Most of the time we want our dogs to be moving at our side, maybe a few feet in front or behind us, but certainly not facing us.

This game teaches your puppy that it pays to come to your side, rather than to your front. It is not intended to teach a perfect heel position. However, the position you teach can certainly be used for having your dog walk nicely by your side when having to bypass distractions such as other people or dogs.

What to do

- Have a few pieces of kibble in your hand, make sure that you have your puppy's attention.
- Use your left hand to lure your puppy past your left leg, let him circle 180 degrees towards you and have him come to a stop next to your leg. This is the position in which you should reward your puppy. Make sure to turn your puppy towards you rather than away from you, so that he will be close to your leg.
- Feed a few more cookies as long as your puppy stays in the position next to you. Every time you feed a cookie, tap your leg with the cookie in your hand first. This is the first step in teaching a visual cue for your dog to come to your side, which can later be used to bypass obstacles.
- For now, it does not matter if your puppy doesn't sit. Standing in that position is fine.
- Repeat the exercise a few times, always remember to tap your leg before you reward the position.

Tips to remember

Always make sure to work on both sides. You may want to teach separate cues for each side. However, I only use one cue and indicate the side by tapping on my leg.

If your puppy tends to swing his butt out when moving into position, start this game next to a barrier such as a wall or fence, until your puppy gains a better understanding for the position that you would like to see.

How to cue

Use a verbal cue for your puppy to come to your side. Additionally, before you feed the treat to your puppy that's in your hand, tap your thigh with the it every time your puppy is in position. This physical cue will be useful later on the agility course.

Stay With Me

OBJECTIVE

Now that your puppy knows to come to your side on cue (even if you still need to help with a lure) and stay there for a while, it is time to add some motion. Your puppy should stay at your side while you are walking, jogging or running, rather than getting in front of your feet.

Again, this game will teach your puppy to follow your motion without getting in the way. Also, it will make your puppy comfortable being close to you, which will be useful in many areas of performance sports later on.

What to do

- Have a few pieces of kibble in your hand and bring your puppy in position next to you.
- Take a small step with the leg which your puppy is next to. If your puppy does not follow automatically, encourage her to follow with your hand. It is important to always take the

step before using your hand as a help. Soon your puppy will anticipate the help and not need it anymore.

- Once your puppy follows your leg movement, you can start to take 2 steps, then 3 and so on. Slowly increase the distance.
- When your puppy is walking next to you for about 15-20 seconds, you can start to challenge her by changing your pace. Move very slowly or jog for a few steps. Remember to reward the new pace a lot before asking for more steps.
- You can further build understanding by adding turns. Start with slight turns away from your puppy, then work your way up to 180 degree turns towards your puppy.

Tips to remember

Always make sure to work on both sides. When walking longer distances, make sure to use a variable reinforcement strategy, this means you should be unpredictable as to when you reinforce. Don't always reinforce after 5 steps for example.

If your puppy tends to swing his butt out when walking, start this game next to a barrier such as a wall or fence, until your puppy gains a better understanding of the position that you would like to see.

Remember, we are not looking for perfect heelwork. The connection between you and your dog is more important than a perfect position.

Tap your leg as often as you can remember before delivering the cookies, even when moving. This will teach a valuable visual cue that will be useful in agility later.

How to cue

Use a verbal cue for your puppy to come to your side. Additionally, tap your thigh with the treat before you feed it every time your puppy is in position. This physical cue will be useful later on the agility course. If your puppy deviates from her position, for example in a turn, you can slap your thigh again to remind her of the position.

Leg Slap

OBJECTIVE

This is a very useful game to built up a skill which can later be used on the agility course. The leg slap lets your puppy know that she is supposed to come to your side and stay there until otherwise instructed. Later, this skill can be used to bypass obstacles in the agility ring, which are not to be taken.

Remember that you were tapping your leg with the piece of kibble before giving it to your puppy in the "come to side" and "stay with me" games? This skill is the reason why!

What to do

- Put your puppy in a control position (stand, sit, down or on a mat) and move away a few feet. Slap your leg and say your verbal cue for coming to side. Reward once your puppy assumes her position. Your puppy should be proficient with this exercise before you continue.
- Put your puppy in a control position. Move a few feet away. Cue the leg slap and start to walk. Reward once your puppy has caught up and moved a few feet with you.
- Repeat the exercise and start making turns away from your puppy, so that she has to follow you on the outside of a small circle that you walk. You can also walk around a cone with your puppy on the outside leg.

- Pick up the pace. First start to jog, then start running. Is your puppy still coming to the correct side? If she tries to cut behind, lower the pace again. This will teach her to stay on the correct side.
- Use distractions. Place a toy close by and recall your puppy past the toy using the leg slap. Once your puppy has passed it, turn around and release your puppy to the toy.
- Place the toy in front of you and your puppy. Release your puppy to the toy a couple times and tug. The third time, move towards the toy with your puppy, but ask for the leg slap and reward your puppy with a different, better toy from your hand.
- You can also use two toys to play this game. Place the toys a few feet apart. Race your puppy to one toy a couple times and play. The next time move towards the first toy, then slap your leg and turn to the second toy. Play with the second toy when your puppy follows you.

Tips to remember

Always work both sides!

As soon as you start using toys or food as a distraction, make sure that you are not always asking your puppy to bypass it, but quite often release her straight to it. Keep things unpredictable.

If your puppy goes straight for the toy when you didn't want her to, make sure to change the setup (i.e. move the toy further away), so that she can be successful the next time. Avoid any "punishment" associated with your puppy choosing the toy. Don't get mad, say "no" or yell. After all, we want a puppy that is happily driving towards the toy! Rather, put the distraction further away or remove it entirely until you have built enough value for your puppy to follow the leg slap.

How to cue

Pick a verbal cue for your puppy to come to your side and stay there. It can be the same cue as you use for walking next to you, or a different one you use only in agility. Anna uses "by", and Daisy uses "check".

The physical cue is a slap on your thigh. You always slap the thigh on the side you want your puppy to be on.

Where's Your Nose?

OBJECTIVE

The objective here for you is to have your dog wipe/swipe at her nose with either front paw. There's no need to ask for any duration here, but do try to reward such that you encourage this swiping at the nose while your puppy is in a sit; it's easier that way for you to see the behavior, and will help keep you from rewarding pawing at the ground, which tends to happen in a down.

You can work on duration later if you like. With puppies, it's not as important that you finish a trick as it is that you START the training for that trick, for the sake of engaging in the learning process with your puppy.

What to do

- **TAPE METHOD:** Put a piece of tape on your puppy's nose and be prepared to mark and reward all the swiping you get! Duct or gaffer tape works well for this; use the smallest amount of tape possible, on the side of your puppy's nose. Your puppy may be so busy pawing that she doesn't notice your cookie, so make sure you put it right to her mouth for this one. Eventually pretend you're putting tape on but don't actually apply anything other than some pressure.

- **BLOW IN THE FACE METHOD:** Gently blow in your puppy's face or on her ears until she shakes her head, and keep blowing until she paws at her face. This is my preferred method, because my verbal cue is "where's your nose?" and I can just accentuate the WH in the word "where", blowing out on to your puppy's face, and in that way the blowing becomes the verbal cue.

Tips to remember

Mark (verbally or with a clicker) as your puppy's paw is making contact with her muzzle/nose, and reward just ABOVE her nose. Be ready to capture this behavior WITHOUT blowing on her face; after just 2-3 very short sessions, your puppy is offering this behavior to the floor vents when there is air coming out and she puts her face over them!

Crawling Backwards

OBJECTIVE

This trick is a great shaping exercise to encourage your puppy to offer behaviors without props around. It increases body awareness and coordination, as your puppy has to focus on how to make the backwards movement happen. Plus, it is a really cute trick!

What to do

- Equip yourself with a clicker and some kibble. Ask your puppy to lie down. Place a piece of kibble between her front paws. As soon as she rocks back the tiniest bit, click.
- Place the reward between your puppy's front paws and click again when she rocks back. Repeat this process a few times.
- After a few rewards, wait to see if your puppy offers to rock back without the help of the kibble. Click and place the reward between the front legs, to encourage further crawling back.
- Wait for more and more crawling before clicking and rewarding.

- When your puppy confidently offers a crawling backwards motion, add the verbal cue of your choice.

Tips to remember

Make sure to never reward your puppy for moving towards you in this exercise. Always reward her towards her own chest, so that you encourage backwards movement. Place the reward on the ground, so that your puppy's head, and thus her whole body, stays in a down position.

How to cue

Try to use only a verbal cue (such as 'scoot'), and no physical cues.

Walk On My Feet

OBJECTIVE

You want your puppy to be comfortable being close to you, and that includes between your legs. This trick requires very little shaping, and can be mostly lured. Plus, it's cute as heck and can be done in a crowded environment, making it an ideal first trick to take "on the road," at shows and the like.

What to do

- With some cookies in hand, reach back through your legs and lure your puppy behind and through your legs so she is facing the same direction as you.
- As you lure your puppy through your legs, move your feet together so that your puppy has to step on your feet as she comes forward. Stop her as she has a foot or feet on your feet.
- As you lure your puppy forward and onto your feet, bring your cookie UP, so that she has to reach up to get to your cookie; this will help her lift her front feet up and get them on your feet.
- As long as your puppy's feet are on your feet, continue feeding.
- Start flexing your toes and even picking up your feet slightly and taking a step forward as you feed.
- When your puppy gets off your feet, stop feeding

- Repeat just a few times and then move on with your day!

Tips to remember

It will be easier for you to be in your stocking feet for this; shoes provide a less stable surface for your puppy than the flat top of your foot, and puppy toenails can be hard on bare feet. As your puppy gets better at moving through your feet to get in position, you can add a verbal cue if you like - luring your puppy through your legs for this trick will also be the beginning step for teaching your puppy to weave between your legs later on.

Turning Left & Right

OBJECTIVE

The idea behind this trick is for your puppy to be able to tell apart his left from his right. It is the foundation of a verbal send to a jump and turning in the direction indicated. It can also be useful for turning your dog off a contact, running or stopped.

This is the first lesson in verbal discrimination that your puppy learns. It teaches her to listen closely to the verbal cue and not blindly offer behaviors, which is a useful soft skill for your puppy to take to the agility course later on.

What to do

- Pick one direction to teach first. Have a piece of kibble in your hand and lure your puppy in a circle to the left or right. Stick with that first direction for now.
- After a few repetition, use your empty hand to lure and reward from your other hand. At this point you should start saying your verbal cue BEFORE you start the hand gesture.
- Try to fade the lure very early on, so that an indication with your finger is enough for your puppy to spin. Always remember to say your verbal cue before using any physical cues.
- Keep working on fading the lure, until your puppy offers the behavior on the verbal cue alone. Now you can start to teach the other direction, but always in separate sessions in the beginning.

- Once your puppy offers both directions on a verbal cue alone, start mixing them up in one session. It is normal for your puppy to struggle with the discrimination at first. Keep sessions short and fun. No more than 10-20 repetitions. Stretch out your training over multiple short sessions each day.
- WORKING POSITIONS: Now that your puppy is confidently spinning in the direction indicated when standing in front of you, slowly rotate a bit with each repetition so that your puppy is standing next to you. Work on 4 scenarios:
    - Puppy standing to your left, turning away from you (turning left)
    - Puppy standing to your left, turning towards you (turning right)
    - Puppy standing to your right, turning away from you (turning right)
    - Puppy standing to your right, turning towards you (turning left)
- Test your puppy's understanding by asking her to turn one direction four times, before throwing in the other direction.
- Increase the level of arousal by playing a game of tug, taking the toy from your puppy and asking for a spin. Keep playing if she spins the in the correct direction.

Tips to remember

Train one direction for a few sessions before starting the other. Work on only one direction per session until you have a solid behavior on the verbal cue alone.

It usually takes quite a lot of repetitions until your puppy can discriminate the two directions on your verbal cues alone. However, the more time you spend on this discrimination now, the fewer repetitions will be necessary on jumps later on.

Try to spend 10-20 cookies a day on left and right turns and you will see progress after a few weeks, rather than obsessing over this behavior.

This is a great little trick to take on the road early on. Try to work on it in many different environments with increasing levels of distraction, as it teaches your puppy to closely listen to your verbal cues even when other things are going on around him.

How to cue

Use a hand gesture at first, but fade it early on. The final behavior should only be a verbal cue, as we want our dogs to be able to discriminate left and right even when we are not close enough to give a physical cue. I use "li" for left and "twiz" for right.

Back Up

OBJECTIVE

Your puppy will walk backwards (not hopping), in a relatively straight line, for at least three steps, and on a verbal cue, without me needing to step in to your puppy physically.

Although you CAN "free shape" this behavior (ie wait for your puppy to back up and then reward by tossing a cookie between her front feet so she backs up even further), try instead to manipulate the environment so that backing up is **likely to happen,** and then you can **CAPTURE** *the behavior.* We like teaching back up this way because it gets your puppy comfortable being in tight spaces, which is helpful for future agility training.

What to do

- Use two objects that your puppy can't climb over or through, or knock over, to make a chute of sorts. Two wings, a crate next to a piece of furniture, two crates, two dog walk ramps tipped on their sides (for small puppies), or something similar will work.

- Lure your puppy forward to the front of the chute you've made, with some food, and then remove the food or close your hand. Make sure you've positioned yourself so that your puppy can't escape by coming FORWARD through the chute.
- When your puppy backs up to get out of the chute you've created, mark and reward quickly by getting the cookies under your puppy's chest and between her front legs, so that she has to lower her head and look under her body a bit to get the cookies. She'll likely take yet another step back to do this, and you can reward THAT too, although her head is now down so you may bonk her on it with the cookie.
- Lure your puppy forward again or call her name to have her come forward again, reward for coming to you at the front of the chute, and then repeat the steps above.

Tips to remember

The longer your chute, the straighter your puppy will back up, BUT, also, the harder it will be for you to lure your puppy forward through the chute.

If your puppy is uncomfortable coming in to the chute, listen to her discomfort, but help her overcome it. Make the chute wider so she is comfortable enough to come forward. If the chute is wide she will probably be able to turn around and won't back up, but that's ok; treat this as a separate behavior at first, the chute, and then work on the backing up separately.

You can also use a cracked door for this if your puppy is not comfortable with her whole body in a chute. Encourage her to poke her head through a door that you're on the other side of, and reward her for poking through. If she comes all the way through and has to push through the door to do this, HOORAY! Reward! And pat yourself on the back for doing some VERY preliminary agility chute training. If she pokes her nose forward and then backs up, you can reward that too, so either way, puppy has fun, learns to be brave nudging objects, and learns to back up a few steps.

Mirror Shake / Wave

OBJECTIVE

When you hold up your right hand to your puppy, just so, she will bring up her left paw to meet your hand. When you hold up your left hand to your puppy, just so, she will bring up her right paw to meet your hand. This trick begins as pawing, and so it will become both the cue for "Shake" as well as "wave".

For "shake", bring your hand in close enough that your puppy can make paw to hand contact. For "wave", you'll hold your hand up the same as for "shake", but the distance will be such that your puppy cannot make paw to hand contact. "Shake" will precede "wave" as a behavior; you will need to work up to hand-to-paw distance in order for shake to become wave.

This behavior also involves more direct "correction" on your part, because the "punishment" for using the wrong paw, or both paws, is that you remove the opportunity for reinforcement entirely, for just a moment, by removing both of your hands in an obvious fashion, to indicate, "try again."

What to do

- First, your puppy has some understanding that a front paw swiping or grasping behavior can earn a cookie. In this case, your puppy has already learned, or started to learn "where's your nose".
- From there, you will have a few cookies in EACH hand. You will take one closed hand, and hold it close to your puppy's mouth/nose, on the same side of your puppy's mouth/nose as your hand. When your puppy paws at your treats with the paw on that side, open the hand quickly to reveal the cookies so your puppy can have them.
- In order to facilitate your puppy reaching for the cookies with a paw and maintaining contact with that paw while your puppy is eating, you may need to bring your hand UP above your puppy's head just a bit, so your puppy is encouraged to lift up on her hind legs to bat at the cookie. A bit of coordination is required, because as your puppy comes DOWN, you want her paw to rest on your hand/arm as she eats the cookies, to reward maintaining contact with you while she's rewarded.
- Once your puppy has done this a few times, even if in a very rudimentary fashion, start to alternate sides. If you work on one side too much, your puppy will continue to try to bat at your hand with the same paw, even if you have switched sides.
- If your puppy makes a mistake, batting at your hand with the wrong paw, or both paws, simply remove your hand, bringing it up close to your chest, and when your puppy settles for a moment, try again, with the same hand, and reward when your puppy is correct.

Tips to remember

It may be useful to start off with OPPOSITE hands, just for a few times, so your puppy gets the idea that paw to hand contact is what is being rewarded. You may want to do a few repetitions of bringing a cookie up, until your puppy comes up off her front paws to reach for the cookie. As she is coming back down, take your non-cookie hand and reach for her paw, continuing to hold it while she eats. Although this ends up being a left-to-right hand-to-paw behavior, once she starts to anticipate that's what you want, and once you see that she is lifting that paw just a teeny bit as she comes up, reaching for your hand, shift gears to follow the steps above in the "what to do" section.

After a few more training sessions, start to bring an index finger up as you hold your hand up toward your puppy. That fist with a raised index finger ends up being your "wave" command. If you hold your hand up and bring it IN to your puppy, flipping your hand so that it is palms up at the very end, when you're close to her, it becomes the "shake" command. If you want to add a verbal cue to either of those behaviors, you can do so AFTER your puppy is reliably performing them on the hand cue. In this way, the hand cue can morph in to the verbal cue.

I can also eventually bring up BOTH hands, when I'm a few feet away, if I want your puppy to bring up BOTH front feet, and in this way, I can begin to teach your puppy to "sit pretty", or "stand", with both front feet in the air. These tricks will be addressed in more detail as "shake" and "wave" become more solid!

Four Feet In The Box

OBJECTIVE

This trick could also be called **FOUR FEET IN THE BOWL**, since I'm going to work toward having your puppy put all four feet in a box OR a bowl that is small enough that the task can only be completed with some difficulty. Your puppy will need to be comfortable with all four feet quite close together under her body in either a bowl or a box for this trick. She'll need to employ core strength to maintain this position, so, at least at first, I won't ask for her to maintain this position for very long. There is a lot of flopping around associated with this behavior, and so this trick is also good for helping your puppy learn to keep trying, even if things are a bit awkward or uncomfortable.

Because this trick requires strength and coordination, it may take some time for a floppy puppy, or a dog of ANY age, to be able to comfortably achieve the four-feet-together stance and maintain it for any length of time. And, dogs of different sizes, lengths, and flexibility levels will have different minimum box/bowl sizes that they can fit into. This, like many of the other behaviors I've taught or am teaching your puppy, may take some time to accomplish and that is totally okay.

What to do

- Start with a box that is large enough with low enough sides that your puppy can comfortably hop in with all four feet. You may want to revisit BEGINNING WITH BOXES. Click/mark and treat when your puppy has all four feet in the box. Ideally, time your mark, whether it is a click or a verbal mark, to the moment that LAST foot makes contact with the floor of the box.
- As your puppy gains confidence and comfort with this behavior, use a smaller box. Make sure that the sides are low enough that your puppy can get in with only a minimum of difficulty, BUT, note that the height of the sides also does give your puppy something to brace against and will be helpful to your puppy. As the sides of the box get lower, your puppy will have to rely on strength and coordination to get and keep all four feet in the box.
- Once you've gotten to a box size where your puppy can comfortably get all four feet in, and maintain all four feet in BUT has to keep all four feet fairly close together, centered under her body, put a food bowl inside the box. The food bowl should be large enough to touch the box on all four sides leaving only the corners of the box free from the edge of the bowl (see image). Continue to work on having your puppy put all four feet in the box/bowl combo. This will further encourage your puppy to put all four feet closely together under her body; she won't want to put her feet in the corners of the box. This will make the task more difficult, BUT, the sides of the box will still be available for her to brace her body against, AND they will also prevent her from sitting in the bowl, which makes it

easier to fit, but doesn't require any strength or coordination.

- As your puppy becomes more capable of moving into the box/bowl combination, remove the bowl from the box periodically and see if your puppy can put four feet JUST in the bowl, without the box. While you're tossing a treat away from the box to "reset" your puppy and get her out of the box to reattempt getting IN, simply move the box behind you and leave only the bowl revealed.

Tips to remember

Your puppy will let you know when she can accomplish this task - don't rush it! She may not have the strength or coordination to do the task quite yet. It may be that, like me, you spend several days at this stage. You can also move the bowl to a corner, so that your puppy has two walls against which she can steady herself. Eventually, your puppy WILL be able to maintain all four feet in a bowl - and at that point, continuing with the exercise as your puppy grows, even with the same size bowl or box, will mean that the difficulty increases, right alongside your puppy's increasing strength, coordination, and balance!

Go To Your Mat

OBJECTIVE

There are all sorts of great reasons to train this particular behavior! Going away from you and toward a mat is basically a "send", where you send your puppy away from you to do an agility obstacle. Going to a mat will help your puppy develop some basic obstacle focus away from you. It will also help you develop a sit or down stay, when the time comes. You can combine BACK UP with GO TO YOUR MAT to encourage your puppy to back away from you further and further or you can simply encourage your puppy to move forward and away from you to go to her mat.

You can also use this behavior as a building block for conditioning behaviors. Finally, this behavior allows YOU to work on your cookie delivery skills, because there is a lot of cookie tossing that is involved with the training. You'll need a mat for this exercise; a rubber-backed bathmat is nice as it won't slip. You need to make sure that the color of the mat contrasts nicely with the color of the surfaces where you'll likely be working on the behavior (a light mat for a dark floor, a dark mat for a light floor, etc.). You'll also want to be sure to keep my mat "special", and only have it down when I want to work on this behavior, at least until your puppy has got the behavior on a verbal cue.

What to do

- First, with this behavior, set up conditions so your puppy is likely to hit the mat, which will be on the floor a few feet away from you. Toss a cookie away from you so that your puppy follows after, and so that when she turns around to come back to you, she passes over the mat. Just as she hits the mat, click (or just mark the behavior verbally) and toss a cookie in front of her on the mat. If the mat is positioned just in front of you, she's likely to stop anyway. If you have a good throw, you can start with the mat a few feet away you.
- Regardless of how close the mat is to you to begin with, start backing away from the mat a bit. Now, marking and tossing that treat as your puppy hits the mat becomes more important! If you don't mark and reward appropriately, your puppy may hit the mat but then continue over the mat to get to you. You need to make sure you take your time backing up, and you need to make sure you have cookies that are appropriate for tossing (they are visible, they won't roll or crumble, etc.)
- Assume that the mat is the center of a clock. In the beginning, you are at 6 o'clock, and your puppy is being sent out to 12 o'clock with a cookie. Then, as she comes back to the center of the clock, she gets rewarded. Once you've backed away from the mat at least a few of your puppy's body lengths, and can see that she understands to stop on the mat, start tossing treats more toward 3 o'clock and 9 o'clock, making it harder for your puppy. Now, she will have to deviate off her return line directly back to you after getting a cookie to hit the mat.

- Finally, when your puppy demonstrates understanding of going to her mat from 3 o'clock and 9 o'clock, work on 6 o'clock. This means your puppy must go AWAY from you to get to the center of the clock. At this point, just as your puppy reaches the mat, give your verbal cue (it can be whatever you like, be creative!)
- BUILDING DURATION: In order to build duration on the mat, simply continue tossing treats onto the mat such that they land in between your puppy's front feet. When you want your puppy to come off the mat, stop tossing treats and before your puppy comes off the mat, say your release word. When she comes off the mat, toss a treat such that she continues off, as you mark the behavior. Since you've already been working on a release to her food bowl, and from her crate, she'll pick up on THIS release fairly quickly. You can work on duration by gradually increasing the amount of time between reinforcements, until there are few/none until the release.
- ENCOURAGING A POSITION: You can choose to encourage a sit, down, or stand on the mat. If you've been working on a sit or down, your puppy may offer one of these positions, and in this case you simply have to reward. However, if you'd like to encourage a down, then mark the behavior of landing on the mat while you're still close to it (early stages) and reward by delivering a cookie between your puppy's two front feet so that she folds back in to a down. If you want a sit, then reward high and back so that she is encouraged to rock back and up into a sit!
- BACKING UP TO THE MAT: Once your puppy understands the behavior of going to a mat, AND how to back up, you can simply pair the two together, by putting the mat behind your puppy so that when you ask her to back up, she hits the mat. Start with just one or two steps back at first, and gradually work up to more!

Tips to remember

Make sure you've got cookies that are good for tossing - they won't crumble, are easily seen, and can be tossed predictably (they don't roll). You may need to get creative if your puppy isn't quite so food motivated. Also, make sure that you build up distance gradually, and that you work on this in short, fun sessions. There's no rush, you've got lots of time, so have fun, and in no time at all your puppy will be happily heading to her mat! You'll have a great landing pad to send your puppy to to keep her from getting underfoot, and you'll have taught her to go to her first obstacle!

Chill On Your Mat (Beginning Stay)

OBJECTIVE

Now that your puppy understands to go to his mat and starts looking for it, it is time to generalize and proof the behavior. Slowly building up duration and distractions will help your puppy to understand that he can relax on his mat, as it is not his turn. This is a very helpful behavior at competitions or seminars, as your puppy is more likely to chill out and not stress about other dogs running around when in his crate or on his mat.

What to do

- Start out with a short reminder: Let your puppy find the mat and reward her for staying on it a few times. If she can stay for about 30 seconds without constantly having to be rewarded, you can proceed to the next step.
- Once your puppy is staying on the mat, move away just one step and then immediately go back to reward.

- Slowly increase the number of steps you move away before going back to reward. If your puppy gets up, you have gone too far. Make sure to reward sooner the next time.
- Once you can move around for a bit with your puppy staying on her mat, start testing the behavior by making sudden movements, jumping, running past the mat, or bringing out a toy. Make sure to reward every successful stay!
- Try dropping a piece of kibble on the floor when your puppy is supposed to stay. Be prepared to cover it fast enough, in case she breaks her stay. In that case, ask a helper to drop the kibble, so that you can focus on rewarding your puppy.
- When your puppy has mastered all those distractions, it is time to bring other dogs into the game. Send your puppy to her mat and have a friend do a trick with her dog. First, the other dog should be further from the mat. With each repetition the dog can move closer and the tricks can be more engaging (include more motion). Maybe your friend can even play with her dog in front of your puppy (who is of course heavily rewarded for staying on her mat).
- Finally, the ultimate distraction is you doing something fun with another dog. For this part it is helpful to have a friend reward your puppy while you engage with another dog. Again, at first ask the other dog for more boring behaviors like sit or down, before you start more engaging tricks or even a game of tug.
- After mastering all these distractions at home, it is time to take the show (mat) on the road. Ask your puppy to go to her mat and stay in different environment. Think about the level of excitement and start out with a more boring place before taking your mat to a trial or agility class.

Tips to remember

Even though your puppy is just relaxing on a blanket, this exercise is hard work for her brain, so try to keep things short and sweet! There is no benefit in trying to train the behavior if your puppy is clearly overwhelmed by the distractions. Try to move away from the distractions until your puppy can be successful. In situations in which your puppy needs to stay somewhere and you are not able to reward appropriately based on her level of understanding, avoid ruining your training progress and rather put your puppy in a crate.

For training with distractions, it can be helpful to use a raised dog bed, so that your puppy has to cross a more clearly defined boundary before breaking the stay.

How to cue

Use your cue for "go to your mat". Don't use an additional wait cue, so your puppy learns to stay on her bed until he is released.

Recognize Your Name (Testing Stay)

OBJECTIVE

This game is especially important for any household that includes multiple dogs. Chances are that sometimes you want to interact with just one of your dogs, while the others should stay out of the way. That means your puppy should learn to recognize when she is called for her turn and when another dog is called and she is supposed to stay. By playing this game your puppy will increase her impulse control.

What to do

- You need your puppy and at least one other dog to play this game. The more dogs you play this game with, the more challenging it gets.
- Put both dogs in a sit or down a few feet away from each other. Move a short distance away and reward your puppy for staying a couple times.
- Now call the other dogs' name and reward him for coming, while walking back to your puppy to reward her for staying. Make sure she is still in position when you reward. She should not get up because she is anticipating the cookie.
- Put the two dogs closer together with each repetition.
- Increase the distance between you and the dogs, so that there is more movement from the other dog running to you.

- Put the other dog behind your puppy, so that he comes running past your puppy from behind. Reward your puppy for staying.

Tips to remember

Don't always call the other dogs first. Sometimes call your puppy first. However, make sure to always reward your puppy for staying when the other dogs are called.

Be creative in how to challenge your puppy further. Can she stay when you call out random words in an exciting tone of voice? Can she stay while the other dog is released to a toy?

How to cue

There's no need to use any physical cues in this exercise, as you want your puppy to learn to stay on a verbal cue alone. Use your verbal wait cue and your puppy's name as a release. Be careful not to use "ok", which would be the general release cue for all the dogs.

Put Your Toys Away

OBJECTIVE

In this multiple stage trick, the final behavior that you are looking for is that your puppy will pick up a ring in her mouth, move it toward and over a box, and then drop it so that it falls into the box. You will need to teach multiple behaviors, and then assemble them together for the final behavior. Because of that, this trick has to be taught in multiple stages, and involves a lot of targeting, as well as purposeful movement of an object from one location to another with the mouth. It requires thinking, and coordination! And, it's fun!

What to do

- STEP ONE: PICK UP A TOY. Use something like the wool ring toy pictured above for this trick. It's soft and fuzzy enough that your puppy can be encouraged to put her mouth on it, but it's not so fuzzy and exciting that she will be enticed to flop it around and shake it a lot. This is important, because you want your puppy to very purposefully put her mouth on the toy so that she can learn to carry it from one location to another. Make sure your puppy is in a playful mood, and then wiggle the ring around just a bit, at mouth level, until she puts her mouth on it, even if just briefly. Then mark/treat. It may be that you have to start with a nose touch to the ring, then go from there to sustained nose contact with the ring, and then an open mouth on the ring. As your puppy gets marked/rewarded for putting her mouth on the toy when it is at or above mouth level, move the toy progressively further down toward the floor, keeping it propped up on its side so that it is easy for her to put her mouth on it. Keep your hand on the toy so that you can feel any pressure she's putting on the toy with her mouth. Mark or reward as she's putting her mouth on the toy and pulling slightly, but before it turns in to a full fledged tug session.

- STEP TWO: GET SOME HEIGHT. You will need to teach your puppy to pick the toy up high enough before she drops it to get it into the toy container. For this trick, your toy container can be a small cardboard box. However, this can pose some problems if you have been working on having your puppy get IN the box, so you need to make sure that you don't reward her for getting in the box herself! As your puppy picks up the toy, delay marking the behavior just a bit, because marking the behavior invariably causes your puppy to drop the toy, knowing a treat is coming. So, delay marking the behavior, AND, when you DO mark the behavior, and your puppy drops the toy to get her cookie, make sure that the cookie is higher than her nose, so that she has to bring her head up further to get it. In this fashion you can gradually get her to lift the toy a bit higher, until it's above the level you need it to be for her to get it into the box.

- STEP THREE: GET THE TOY NEAR THE BOX. Here's where your skill with placement of reinforcement really pays off. Your puppy already views the box as a target, because you have taught her at least a couple of behaviors with the box (such as getting IN the box). But, you need to teach her now that the goal is to take the ring, pick it up, and move it toward and ultimately drop it IN the box. You need to let her know that the goal is to decrease the distance between the ring and the box. So, as she is being rewarded for picking up the ring, bring the box into the picture, off to the side. And, each time that she picks up the ring, mark but then REWARD **in the direction of the box**. This is important! Once you've got your puppy bringing the ring near to the box, MOVE the box, so that she sees that the goal is always to get the ring closer to the box, and not just to a bit of geography in front of where you're sitting.

- STEP FOUR: PUT THE TOY IN THE BOX. Once your puppy understands that the goal is to get the toy near the box, continue rewarding high, but OVER the box (or beyond it on the other side), to encourage her to be aiming for the box with the ring. amove the box as needed to encourage her to remember that the goal is to bring the toy TO the box, and then deliver your reward in such a fashion so that she anticipates always getting it over (or even IN) the box. As you approximate this you'll be shaping her aim, so that she aims to drop the toy IN the box!

Tips to remember

Remember that you want your puppy to pick up and move the toy, and not fling it. Try not to reward any flinging. Use a less interesting toy, or hold on to it with your hand at first to encourage just a mouth on that toy. Also, you want your puppy to move that toy, like the mechanical arm in that machine at the arcade where you try to get the toy, right? You want height, and movement, in small increments, from the location of the toy to the location of the box.

You may need to move the box so that your puppy gets the idea that movement of the ring isn't randomly rewarded, it's rewarded if the ring gets closer to the box. Also, don't forget to reward high enough to encourage your puppy to come UP with that toy. Once your puppy gets the toy IN the box, even if it's accidental, make sure you give a HUGE reward, and give the reward **in the box**. This way your puppy gets to see, actually see, the picture of her head, in the box, with the toy at the bottom of the box. And then, you can teach your puppy to take the toy OUT of the box!

Circling A Cone

OBJECTIVE

With this behavior, you're going to go through a step-by-step process to teach your puppy to turn away from you and circle a cone. This particular behavior is a great way for you as a trainer to explore the concepts of "zone clicking" and placement of reinforcement. It's also a fun trick to train that has broader applications in agility (weave poles, rear crosses at jumps, and bending around a jump standard, to name just a few!). First though, a little background information is required. (*This material first appeared in Clean Run Magazine as a 10-minute trainer article, and then as part of my 10-minute trainer ebook. It has also appeared in Linda Mecklenburg's MASTERING JUMPING SKILLS book as an Appendix - so it's an important behavior!*)

WHAT IS ZONE CLICKING?

Zone clicking, in short, is the idea that rather than clicking in the exact same place at the exact same time for each attempt, you'll purposefully vary when and where you click for behavior, with a "zone", so that the dog does not know exactly when and where the click will come.

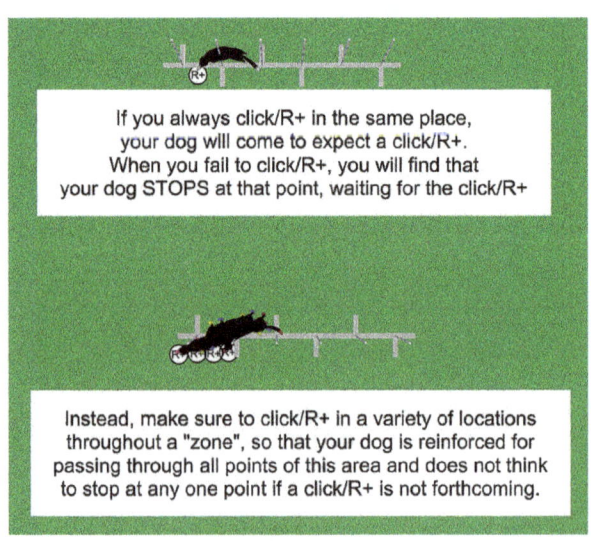

FIGURE 1

Because your puppy is reinforced for moving through a zone rather than a single point, your puppy is less likely to stop and wait if a click is not forthcoming. Instead, your puppy will continue traveling through the zone in hopes of getting you to click. The weave poles are a great example of the need for zone clicking; if you always click at the exact same time and place as your dog exits the poles, then, when you FAIL to click at that moment, you will find that your dog STOPS dead in his tracks!

With weave pole training, you want to click as your dog moves through the zone between poles 11-12, rather than at the same time and place each time (if you use a clicker at all for this behavior). In each case in Figure 1, the dog is clicked at the point marked R+, and the reinforcement is delivered ahead of the dog's path to encourage the dog to continue forward out of the poles.

WRAPPING THE CONE

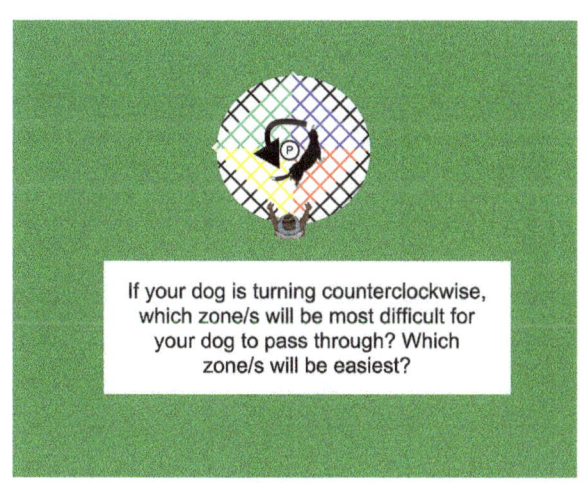

FIGURE 2

When it comes to teaching your puppy to wrap a cone, think of the cone as being in the center of a circle, and divide the circle in to four zones. Take a look at Figure 2.

Let's say you want to teach your puppy to turn counterclockwise around a cone. Which zone do you think will be the most difficult for your dog to move through? Which zone will likely be the easiest for your puppy to move through? You will need to plan on giving more reinforcements to your puppy for moving through difficult zones, and fewer reinforcements for moving through those zones that are already easy for your dog.

For most puppies, the red zone will be the most difficult zone to pass through, as the dog will need to turn away from you (the source of most of the dog's reinforcement!), and toward the cone. The blue zone will be next in terms of difficulty, as your puppy continues to turn away from you and toward the cone. Once your puppy gets to the green zone, however, he is on his way BACK to you, and so this zone, along with the yellow zone, tends to be the easiest zone for your puppy.

This means that as a trainer, you will be looking to click the most as your puppy passes through the red zone, and reinforce the most in the blue zone, at least at first. However, this does not mean you will not click or treat for the other zones as well; just not as much as those zones you deem more difficult. As you progress through teaching this behavior, you may find that the difficult zones change for your puppy, and you should be prepared to shift how and when you click and treat as you see one zone becoming easier and another more difficult.

What does this mean for you as the trainer?

In order to help your puppy become more comfortable moving through the red zone, you will need to click at various points within that zone, always delivering the reward (food) ahead of your dog in the NEXT zone (again, not always in the

C1 corresponds to click #1, and R1 is where the treat would be delivered for click #1. C2 is for click #2, and R2 is where the corresponding treat would be delivered, and so on and so on.

FIGURE 3

same PLACE within that zone). Split each zone in to even smaller sections, and make sure that you are clicking for multiple points within each zone, and delivering your reinforcement to corresponding multiple points in the NEXT zone. See Figure 3 for an example.

Be smart about your hands

Although this is a shaping and offering behavior, you are still a variable, and the way you deliver each reinforcement can help or hinder your puppy's ability to get reinforcement for future attempts. In the counterclockwise example, as the dog passes through the red zone, and as I click and attempt to deliver a treat in the blue zone, I need to think carefully about which arm and hand I will use to deliver the treat. After all, after I drop the treat on the ground, I must retract my arm, and the motion of that retraction will serve as a lure. So, will I use my left arm or my right arm in this case? See Figure 4a and 4b.

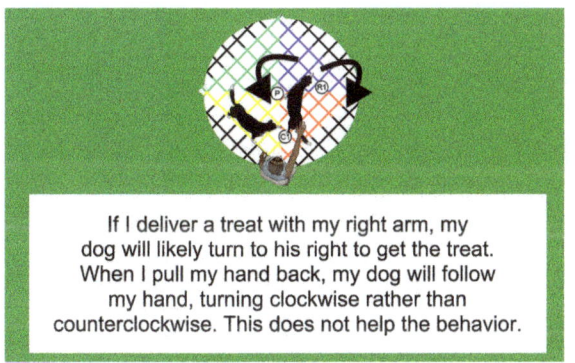
If I deliver a treat with my right arm, my dog will likely turn to his right to get the treat. When I pull my hand back, my dog will follow my hand, turning clockwise rather than counterclockwise. This does not help the behavior.

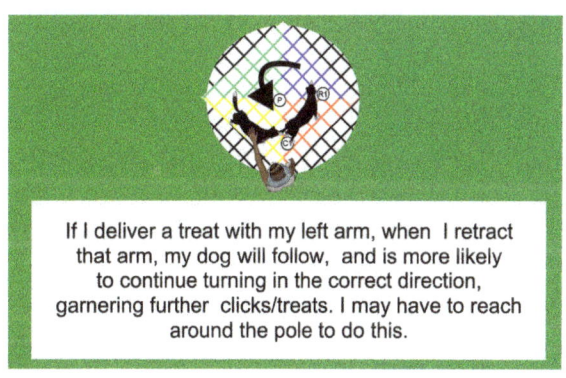
If I deliver a treat with my left arm, when I retract that arm, my dog will follow, and is more likely to continue turning in the correct direction, garnering further clicks/treats. I may have to reach around the pole to do this.

FIGURE 4A AND 4B

You can't eliminate yourself as a lure entirely, so instead, be smart about HOW you lure. Do try to get your hand out to deliver the treat as quickly as possible, and pull it back as quickly as possible (don't lure your puppy around the post with a cookie in your hand!!), but be clever about which hand you use so your puppy is not encouraged to turn the wrong way.

Reward all zones…with one exception.

Although the red and blue zone may be the more difficult zones in this case (and don't forget to also teach your dog to circle the OTHER way!), you should still reward your dog for passing through each and every zone on the circle, with one exception.

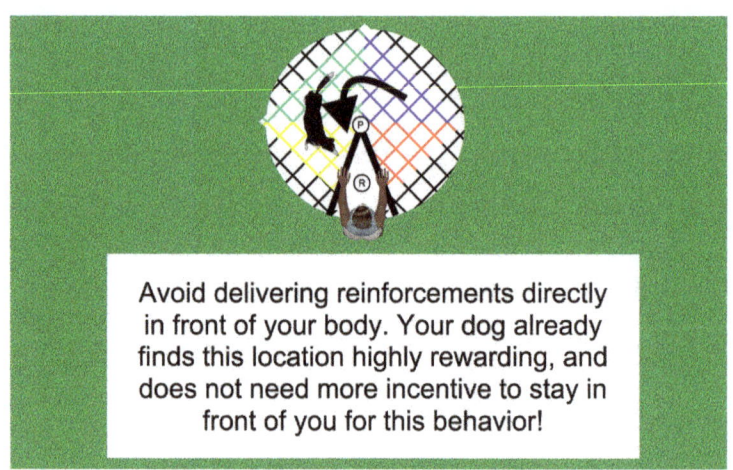

Avoid delivering reinforcements directly in front of your body. Your dog already finds this location highly rewarding, and does not need more incentive to stay in front of you for this behavior!

FIGURE 5

As your puppy has already been very highly rewarded at your front, from the time he first came in to your life, you should avoid delivering reinforcements directly in front of your body, until your dog has become proficient at the behavior. For many puppies, once they have received a cookie at the handler's front, there is too much value in staying at that location, and too little value in turning away. The puppy will often start to offer a variety of other behaviors at that point, rather than continuing on through the space in front of the handler. See Figure 5.

Start small, then ask for more

In the beginning, be prepared to click and treat five, six, or even seven or more times as your puppy travels around the cone. You will need to be quick! You want to build value for each and every point around that cone. Don't ask your puppy to travel through more space than he is comfortable traveling through, or you will create hesitant and slow circling. You will find almost immediately that the "easy" zones will not require as much reinforcement, and so while you will continue to reinforce in those zones, the pieces of the pie that your puppy will have to travel through will quickly become larger.

For the difficult zones, you'll want to maintain a high level of reinforcement, taking care to vary where your clicks and treats are delivered throughout the zones, rather than in the same place each time. You've worked hard to be precise prior to this point, and now, you must be precisely variable with your clicks and treats!

Practice before you train!

Because delivery of the reinforcement is so important, practice how you'll deliver reinforcement before you get your puppy out to do your training! Once again, what is learned here has broader applications to your agility training. Will you practice throwing your reinforcement before you start weave pole training? Will you practice the delivery of your reinforcement, without your puppy, prior to your contact training? Would the training of those, or any other behavior, be improved if you practice beforehand?

Ipsilateral (Side Foot) Targeting

OBJECTIVE

This is a trick, but also requires some strength and coordination. Your puppy has been learning to back up, and to target an object with her back feet, but hoisting her back feet up higher, on to a wall, or a board that is angled up against a wall, requires more conditioning and also can potentially place more unnatural force on your puppy's body. So, while you may want to teach this trick, be careful not to overdo it! This trick is a variant of putting two REAR feet on a wall or a board, in that you want your puppy to put her two left or her two right feet on a wall or a board.

What to do

- Use a board angled up against the wall, with a non-slip surface. After a couple of repetitions of having your puppy put her two BACK feet on the surface, reorient yourself and your puppy so that she is parallel to the wall instead of perpendicular to it.
- Using cookies, reward your puppy for putting a back foot on the wall, just as she had been doing previously. However, while you would reward low and in front of her nose for two BACK feet, keep your cookies high enough now that she CAN'T put her other back foot on the board. Instead, encourage her to lift her head and front foot up on the same side, to put THAT foot on the board, to get the cookie.

- Now your puppy has BOTH feet on one side of her body on the board! Praise as you let your puppy eat the treats, and then toss a cookie away from the board to reset and start again.
- Do this just a couple of times on each side, and then move on.

Tips to remember

This is a fairly simple behavior to work on IF you have already been working on teaching your puppy to back up to an object. If not, work on that behavior first. Remember to use something that has a nice, grippy surface, and is stable; you can progress to using a fitness peanut or ball later, when your puppy is more coordinated, and physically ready for this exercise!

Discriminating Behaviors

OBJECTIVE

When thinking of what is asked of our dogs in any sport, there is always the need for them to discriminate different behaviors on verbal cues. For this reason, it is useful to teach your puppy to listen closely to what you are saying. After all, physical cues are much more natural for dogs to understand. That is why it is beneficial to teach them to listen to verbal cues early on. Just think about a contact tunnel discrimination in agility. Chances are you can't always be there to help your dog with your physical cues.

What to do

- Send your puppy to her mat or a raised bed. Since you have created lots of value her to stay there, chances are good that you can add some distance early on. Start with just a couple feet.
- Ask your puppy for behaviors she already knows pretty well. Start with the discrimination of two behaviors, for example sit and down.
- Your puppy should be able to switch between these two behaviors pretty easily, after all if it is not one, it must be the other. So you can add a third behavior. Personally, I like to use left and right once they are trained on a verbal cue alone.
- Start mixing in more and more behaviors, rewarding your puppy for each correct response.

- Increase the distance to the mat or bed, so that your puppy will learn to respond to your cues at a distance.
- After you have played this game a few times and your puppy understands how to execute the behaviors on the verbal cue at a distance, you can try some easy discrimination without a mat. Make sure to never reward your puppy for coming towards you, but always toss the cookie or go towards your puppy.

Tips to remember

When working on this, make sure your puppy is actually waiting for the verbal cue and not just randomly offering behaviors that were reinforced recently. From time to time, wait a few more seconds than usual and reward your puppy for being still and waiting for a cue.

When working at a distance, make sure to reward your puppy on the bed or mat, not when she is coming towards you. Raising the mat helps with this in the beginning. You can also toss your reward on the mat.

How to cue

Use whatever verbal cues you have taught for the behaviors you are asking for. Be aware that we often use physical cues unintentionally. If you are not sure, ask a friend to watch for unintentional physical cues or video yourself.

Tug Think Tug

OBJECTIVE

This game gives you the chance to work on your drop it cue. Your puppy will learn to voluntarily and quickly drop her toy in order to do a trick before she can tug again. This serves as a first introduction to thinking while in a higher state of arousal, which is important for many aspects of the dog performance world later on. Additionally, this is a great game to speed up the performance of a certain behavior.

What to do

- Play a game of tug with your puppy. Tell her to release the toy and take it from her.
- Ask your puppy to perform a behavior she knows well, for instance a sit or a down.
- As soon as your puppy hits the position you asked for, release her and reward with playing tug again.

- After rewarding the same behavior a few times, try a different behavior.
- You may also want to try tricks like hand bobs or spinning.

Tips to remember

This is an exhausting game for your puppy, as it involves playing and thinking! Keep sessions short and sweet, don't go overboard.

When you ask your puppy to drop the toy, make sure to hold it still so she is less enticed by it.

If your puppy is unable to perform the behavior you asked for, give her more time after first tugging activity to calm down, then repeat the cue.

Don't keep repeating your verbal cue if your puppy doesn't respond! This will only spoil your cues. Rather, try to set her up so she can be successful in the next repetition (less intense play, lower arousal, more time after tugging to calm down, use behavior she understands well).

How to cue

You can use behaviors that you have trained on a verbal cue or on a physical cue in this game. For drop it I use a verbal cue only.

Listening When Aroused

OBJECTIVE

The idea behind this game is to further improve impulse control and, more importantly, to teach your puppy to listen and respond to your verbal cues under higher levels of arousal. When teaching a behavior, we have been working in a low-arousal environment.

However, your puppy should know some behaviors well enough by now for us to check if she can still do them under higher arousal. After all, performance dogs need to be able to execute all kinds of behaviors under very high levels of arousal. So this is a valuable exercise to teach them to think in the face of excitement.

What to do

- Have treats and a toy ready. Ask your puppy to offer to be restrained, then toss a toy a few feet away.
- Watch your puppy to see if she is ready to respond to a verbal cue. If she is struggling to go after the toy, wait for her to calm down.

- Give your verbal cue. You should choose a behavior she knows really well, for example a sit or down.
- As soon as your puppy executes that behavior, release her to the toy.
- Repeat this game with different behaviors.
- Increase the level of arousal by playing tug before throwing the toy or by building up some excitement using your "reeeady, steeeady" cue.

Tips to remember

It is very difficult for your puppy to respond to you in a state of high arousal! Don't get mad if she is not successful yet. Make sure she really understands the behavior in a state of low arousal. Then slowly increase the arousal. Maybe you can use a less exciting toy or food? Check your top ten rewards list and work your way up from the bottom.

Only use behaviors your puppy understands really well. Stationary behaviors are easier than non-stationary behaviors, so save your left and right for a later session.

Make sure to reward your puppy for taking the position you asked for, as that is the most difficult part. This is not a stay exercise! If you ask for a sit, release as soon as your puppy's butt hits the ground.

How to cue

Use whatever verbal cues you have taught for the behaviors you are asking for. Release your puppy to the toy with "Ok, get it" after she has successfully executed the behavior.

Conditioning For Puppies

THE CASE FOR STARTING YOUNG

When your puppy is 4-5 months old, start introducing her to some conditioning exercises. She's already been doing a lot of off leash hiking, swimming, and running around, so she **does** have some muscle tone, and a baseline level of fitness. However, be careful to keep conditioning exercises age appropriate. First and foremost, they must be FUN for your puppy, and for you, or neither one of you will want to continue. However, any conditioning exercises started now must also be SAFE and age appropriate. You want to be able to work on conditioning and toning exercises one tiny bit at a time, so that over TIME, the strength, coordination, and flexibility that your puppy will need to start and continuing doing agility will be achieved. But, you don't want to put any undue or repetitive stress on puppy bones, muscles, tendons, ligaments, joints, etc., that may put your puppy at risk for injury.

We're not all that regimented when it comes to conditioning training; we prefer the "a little of this, a little of that" approach, and, over time, hitting ALL the areas.

Transferring Left & Right to Wings

OBJECTIVE

Remember a while back, you taught your puppy to spin to the left and to the right on a verbal cue alone? Now it is time to transfer that behavior to jump wings. The purpose of this is to teach your puppy strong sends that will be super helpful on the agility course later. Strong sends allow your adult dog to commit to a jump early on, while you can already move towards the next obstacle.

This will help you to be in a good position to handle the next line and your dog to know early on that he is turning. A good discrimination between left and right will further help you to prevent injuries, because your dog is less likely to jump in the wrong direction and land inappropriately. When cues are timely, your left and right will be essential in keeping your dog on track and helping him to know where he is going early on.

What to do

- Remind your puppy of the 4 scenarios you have taught in the previous lesson on this topic:

- Puppy standing to your left, turning away from you (turning left)
- Puppy standing to your left, turning towards you (turning right)
- Puppy standing to your right, turning away from you (turning right)
- Puppy standing to your right, turning towards you (turning left)

• Now position your puppy in between two jump uprights that are sitting so close together, that they are almost touching your puppy. Ask your puppy to turn and reward if he circles the upright. If he spins in place, it is okay to lure him around the upright the first couple times. Fade the lure quickly though.

• Work all 4 scenarios once your puppy understands to include the upright in his circle.

• Incrementally, move the starting position backwards. Your puppy should now take a step through the uprights before turning, then two steps, three steps and so on. Again, working all 4 scenarios.

• Slowly move the uprights apart, until they have the regular distance, so that a jump bar fits in between. Again, work all 4 scenarios.

Tips to remember

Make sure to work all 4 scenarios for every step.

For the first steps, it is easier to use a wingless upright, before using wings. If you don't have jumps, you can also use sticks in the ground, cones or water bottles.

These steps take time! Plan to spend a few sessions on each step: transferring to uprights, changing the starting position and increasing the distance between the uprights. The more time you allow your dog to UNDERSTAND this exercise now, with limited speed, the fewer repetitions will he need on the actual jump.

This is not a speed exercise, but a thinking game. It is more important that your puppy looks for the correct direction to turn, than for him to run fast. Speed will be added at a later point.

How to cue

Use your verbal cues from spinning left & right. Be careful to avoid any physical cues such as using your hands. This should be trained on verbal cues alone.

Testing Understanding Of Left & Right

OBJECTIVE

After transferring your left & right turns to wings, it is now time to test your puppy's understanding. This is important to help them improve their listening skills. By playing this game you expose your puppy to many different approaches and situations he will likely encounter when running courses later on. These exercises will improve his confidence to handle such situations, as he will already be familiar with them.

What to do

- **Changing the angle:** Once your puppy is confident being sent to a wing in all 4 scenarios, it is time to change the angle of approach. Slowly, move your puppy's starting position from straight to more angled. Again, ask for all 4 scenarios, so that your puppy also has to bend away from you while you are approaching the wing parallel.
- **Adding motion:** First, add only some motion while working on angles that are easier for your dog. Then increase your speed and slowly make the angle of approach more difficult again. With your increased pace, your dog is also likely to increase his speed. Be on the watch for wider turns and do not reward those.

- **Adding speed:** Increase your puppy's speed by using a toy to reward him. Restrain your puppy before you ask for left or right, release as soon as you see commitment in your puppy. Pull a toy on a string away from your puppy to encourage him to power out of the turn.

Tips to remember

Before starting this exercise, it is important to consider your puppy's development. Do not start this game when your puppy is still too young! There is no absolute age that dictates when to start. Consider your puppy's breed, size, weight and structure. If in doubt, check with your vet before doing these exercise.

Even if you deem your puppy ready for these kind of physical exercises, don't overdo it in the number of repetitions! Keep sessions short and fun!

Make sure to work all 4 scenarios for every step.

Work in small steps when changing the angle. Add motion and speed carefully. First walk, then jog and finally run.

If your puppy fails to turn in the correct direction or to commit to the jump entirely, decrease the distance and make the angle of approach easier. Only raise one criteria at a time, either angle, your motion or your puppy's speed. Don't ask for too many things at once.

How to cue

Use your verbal cues for turning left and right from the previous exercise. Be careful to avoid any physical cues such as using your hands. This should be trained on verbal cues alone.

The Bang Game

OBJECTIVE

The bang game is one of the first things that you might do with your puppy on a "real" piece of agility equipment. It's not something that we spend a lot of time on, or do that frequently, because when we DO play the bang game, we put a LOT of enthusiasm in to it, and a ton of energy. Usually, when we're done playing the bang game even for a minute or so, our throats are hoarse from vocalizing just how exciting we think this game is!

There are three basic elements to the seesaw: The sound, the height, and the movement The bang game is a way to get your puppy comfortable with the first of those three elements, the sound. By putting your puppy in control of making the noise, you can make sure she is confident around the obstacle, AND by pumping a lot of enthusiasm into your efforts, you can also condition your puppy to get excited just by hearing the seesaw banging, even if she's not the one banging it!

It's not important HOW your puppy bangs the seesaw at this point. She can grab it with one paw, she can jump on it, she can ricochet off of it. Any interaction with the end of the board that results in the board making any sound as it hits the ground will be enthusiastically rewarded, and from there, the louder your puppy bangs that board, the more enthusiastic the reward will be. And, since you've been working with your puppy getting in a box, in a bowl, on mats and boards, on perches, and other similar objects, the concept of getting ON something for a reward is not a new one for your puppy.

What to do

- Set up the seesaw so that it's just a few inches from the ground. You can prop the low end up with a jump upright, a table, or a chair, or you can just hold the high end down with a leg so that it's a few inches above the ground.
- Using your puppy's favorite food or toy, encourage your puppy to interact with the board. If your puppy is tentative, then the board should just BARELY be off the ground, and even if it only very quietly hits the ground, reward! If your puppy is confident, the board can be a few inches above the ground, but remember, even a confident puppy can be easily startled, so it's better to work up to more height, which will produce a louder bang.
- As soon as the board hits the ground, praise effusively and move AWAY from the seesaw as you praise, and KEEP praising. Your praise should take 10x longer than the actual bang did! You'll want to move away from the seesaw as you do this so that your puppy isn't startled by the seesaw returning to its resting position. And, if you're like me, and you just propped the seesaw down with a leg, it's going to bang AGAIN, as it reaches its final resting position, and you can reward AGAIN for the bang.

Tips to remember

Always make sure that it is your puppy's choice to interact with the seesaw. If your puppy is skeptical about the seesaw, or you anticipate some skepticism, work up to the bang game gradually. Make sure that your puppy gets to see the seesaw in action prior to

actually interacting with it. If you're alone but have another dog, crate your puppy within sight and work on the seesaw with that other dog. Or, in a class situation, or at a show or fun match, reward your puppy each time another dog makes the seesaw bang. You can also teach your puppy tricks that make noise, such as closing a door, or a cupboard or a drawer with her paws, so that she gets accustomed to making noises with objects.

As your puppy gains confidence with the bang game, use some restraint to generate even more enthusiasm. Hold your puppy back from the lowered seesaw end, start getting her excited, and when she starts to pull and lean toward the seesaw, let go of her, and be ready to reward, reward, reward when she makes that bang!

Introducing The Tunnel

OBJECTIVE

When your puppy is 4-5 months old, introduce her to the tunnel. This introduction is not to be confused with full blown training of the tunnel. Instead, as the title indicates, it's just an introduction. Your only objective at this point is to give your puppy some positive experiences with the obstacle. You probably won't do any real handling associated with this obstacle for some time, until your puppy is more mentally and physically ready.

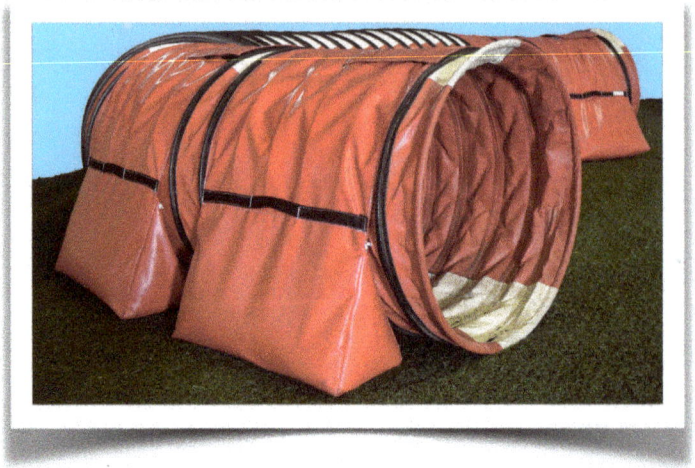

What to do

There are a few different ways you can introduce your puppy to a tunnel.
- You can start with a short, straight tunnel, have a helper hold your puppy, go to the other side, and excitedly call her through. To start, crouch at the other end of the tunnel and actually call your puppy through such that she can see you. Then, crouch but face forward rather than facing toward your puppy. Then, gradually stand up, facing forward, on the opposite end of the tunnel. As your puppy comes through the tunnel, praise

verbally with enthusiasm, run away a short distance to encourage your puppy to chase you, and either reward with food or toys when she catches you.

- If your puppy is not as adventurous at that particular moment, you can start much smaller, and click/treat for your puppy approaching, examining, and then interacting with and going through the tunnel. Again, the tunnel should be very short, with no curve to start. As your puppy comes out of the tunnel, run away a short distance to encourage your puppy to chase you, and either reward with food or toys when she catches you.
- Or, you can have your puppy chase another dog through the tunnel. As long as the dog that your puppy is chasing is "safe" (ie., won't turn around and mistake your puppy for a squeaky toy), you can let your prey-driven puppy chase after another dog as it goes through the tunnel. You may need to restrain your puppy just a bit, to give the other dog a head start, AND encourage your puppy to go through the tunnel rather than meet the adult dog at the exit (beware of the smart puppy who does this!!).

Tips to remember

Regardless of the method you choose, if there is any restraint involved to help generate enthusiasm for the tunnel, make SURE that you do not EVER push your puppy forward as you release her. There should ONLY be pulling back and letting go. Just like trying to put a cat in a box, if you push your puppy forward, you will **decrease** her desire to go toward the object you're pushing her toward. Restraint and release.

You should use a straight short tunnel to start, if you're choosing one of the first two methods. I tend to use the third method, if I can see that my puppy is motivated to chase. It's pretty exciting, and allows me to be a bit lazier and use the tunnels as they already lay in my arena, without having to shift them. Even then, I am prepared to back up to a straight short tunnel when I do decide to see if my puppy will go through **without** another dog to chase. And, even if my puppy goes IN to a tunnel chasing another dog, I prefer it to be ME that your puppy chases when she comes **out** of that tunnel. I'll give my adult dog a head start while I restrain my puppy, and then release my puppy to go through the tunnel. When my puppy comes out, I'll be prepared to run and have a toy at the ready for her to chase after. Usually, the adult dog is happy to come out of the tunnel and watch the entertainment behind him.

With this introduction, there's no need to work on any real handling. No rear crosses, no odd angles to the tunnel entrance, and not much repetition. This is just an introduction, and you may not even come back to it for several weeks or more. In the meantime, your puppy will have had plenty of time to watch all of the excitement of your other dogs (and dogs at the competitions) going through tunnels!

Turning Away To A Tunnel

OBJECTIVE

Once you've introduced your puppy to a tunnel, you'll want to start showing your puppy all of the subtleties associated with HOW you might ask her to perform the obstacle. If you wait until your puppy has done many, many tunnels the 'logical' way (see figure A), it will be more difficult to then illustrate to your puppy that you want her to take the tunnel even when your location and motion may NOT be logical, as in Figure B.

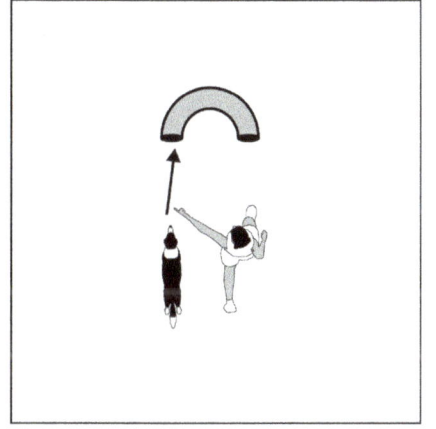

Figure A (left): This is a more logical presentation of the tunnel, because the handler is located such that the dog can curve with the tunnel and come back to the handler.

Figure B (right): This is a less logical presentation of the tunnel, because the handler is located such that the dog has to curve away from the handler to go through the tunnel. Most dogs will realize that the tunnel in figure B curves to the left, but in order to come back to the handler they must be on their right lead, and will either not do the

tunnel, or will spin at the entry and come back out.

In this lesson, you simply want to teach your puppy the beginnings of turning away from you to take a tunnel when you (the tunnel, the dog, and you) are arranged as shown in figure B. You will also count the training that follows to be the very beginning of training landing side approaches (threadles) for your dog on jumps and tunnels.

What to do

- First, send your puppy through the chosen tunnel, arranged as shown in Figure A above. Do this in both directions, and as your puppy is going through the tunnel, remain in a central location, and reward your puppy with food or toys when she comes out.
- After you have sent your puppy through the tunnel as shown in Figure A, then, with your hand in your puppy's collar, hold her very close to a tunnel as shown below in Figure C, and restrain her, and when SHE pulls forward to take the tunnel, release her.
- As your puppy heads in to the tunnel, step in behind her, so that when she comes out, you're once again in a central location, ready to reward her when she comes out.
- Do this in BOTH directions. Start using a verbal cue as soon as your puppy is reliably going in to the tunnel. This verbal cue is NOT the same cue that you will use to cue your dog to take a tunnel when we are arranged as shown in figure A.
- NEXT STEPS: As your puppy gains proficiency with

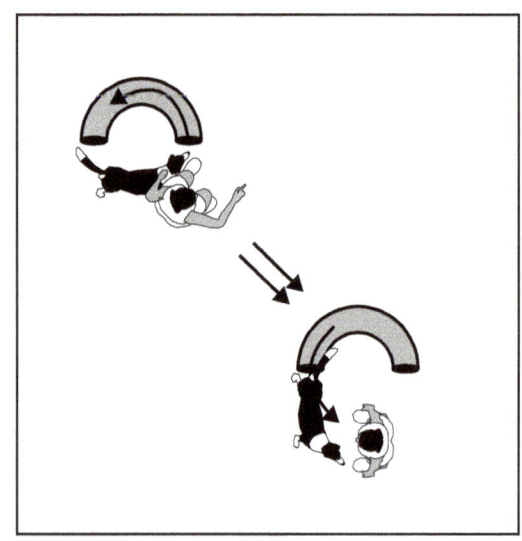

Figure C

this behavior, straighten the tunnel and start to work on a little bit of distance *from the tunnel entry, but not from the tunnel itself.* See Figure D. Once you have changed location as shown in Figure D, at some point (as your puppy's commitment to the behavior increases) work on distance from the tunnel itself, rather than just from the entry of the tunnel.

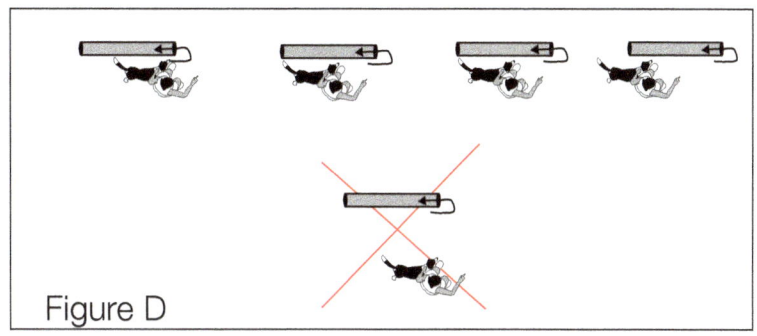

Figure D

Bypassing A Tunnel

OBJECTIVE

Everyone has seen a tunnel sucker on an agility course before - a dog who loves taking tunnels so much, that the handler has trouble keeping their dog from shooting off into a tunnel. That is why it is important to teach your puppy that taking a tunnel is not always the correct choice, after having spent so much time to get her excited about taking tunnels.

What to do

- First, remind your puppy of the leg slap you have taught. Remember to use your verbal as well as physical cue.
- Repeat the game in which you run towards a toy with your puppy, but ask her to follow you with the leg slap rather than letting her go straight for the toy.
- Now replace the toy with a tunnel. At first, put your puppy in a control position a few yards from the tunnel. Position yourself between the tunnel and your puppy, closer to your puppy. Release your puppy and ask for the leg slap. You should turn away from the tunnel and your puppy should follow.
- With each repetition, move yourself closer to the tunnel before releasing your puppy, until you can be standing right in front of the tunnel and your puppy still follows your leg slap.

- Now slowly add motion. Start out further from the tunnel, before you move closer again, now moving towards the tunnel with your puppy.
- Finally, run towards the tunnel. Move past it while doing your leg slap. Your puppy should follow you.
- Play this game both with straight as well as curved tunnels.

Tips to remember

Always remember to work both sides!

Don't get angry if your puppy takes the tunnel by mistake. Rather, make sure to set her up for success in the next repetition. Increase the distance to the tunnel or decrease your motion. Make sure to heavily reward your puppy for following you. We built a lot of value for the tunnel, so it is not surprising that your puppy has a strong drive to it. We want to keep that strong drive, but at the same time make sure your puppy also has a strong desire to follow your movement.

On average, every third repetition, you should ask for (and reward) the tunnel rather than the leg slap. Don't pattern your puppy. Always make sure she is thinking and paying attention and not blindly doing what she has done for the last three repetitions. Keep things exciting and unpredictable.

How to cue

Use your physical and verbal cue you have used before for the leg slap. Make sure to cue it on whichever side you want your puppy to be on.

Final Thoughts

Anna and I hope that you have enjoyed this book, and that you have gotten a lot of use out of it. Hopefully, it is dog-eared, with pencil markings and notes scribbled in the margins. While there are plenty of online options for dog training these days, I find that having a physical book in hand is invaluable. You can toss it in your training bag, keep it handy for reference, and refer to it again and again, with each new puppy that finds its way in to your home and heart.

While there's a lot of material in this book that will keep you and your puppy busy for quite some time, there are countless other things that you can do with your puppy to help develop him or her into the best possible performance partner for your chosen sport. Even though I myself have raised multiple performance puppies for agility, I find that with each new puppy, I have that "deer in the headlights" feeling when it comes to what I should do with respect to training. I, like many of you, feel a sense of anxiety and some pressure to "get it right." However, in the end, the most important thing is to **enjoy the process**. And so, I return to that thought again and again.

Of course I have some outcome oriented goals in mind with my puppy, but those goals won't be worth achieving if we haven't enjoyed the process of achieving them together, as a team. So, while it is my sincere hope that all of the activities in this book help you to develop your puppy in to a wonderful teammate, you should also recognize that this book is a resource, but not an all-inclusive one! NOT doing all of the activities in this book doesn't spell disaster for you and your puppy! This book should give you ideas, and plenty of them, about all of the different activities you can do with your puppy.

You and your puppy have a lot of learning to do about one another. Your puppy may not even really know who he or she is yet. Of course you will play a large role in developing just who your puppy becomes! Don't be afraid to be flexible, and to adapt the exercises and activities in this book to more appropriately suit you and your individual puppy. There are a lot of generalizations we can make about our puppies, but at the end of the day, each puppy is a unique individual, with needs, wants, desires, and yes, even fears and things they would rather avoid.

Your puppy has his or her own timeline, and while I do like to keep things moving forward, with respect to training, rushing a puppy is never productive. Take your time, and let your puppy be the one to tell you how quickly to progress with a given activity or exercise, or how long to linger before moving on. The most important thing is to **have fun**, and **enjoy the process.** Your puppy won't be a puppy for very long, and before you know it, he or she will be an adolescent, and then an adult! Have fun, and enjoy the ride.

~ Daisy Peel

About This Book

This content is intended solely for the purchaser and is not for redistribution. Obviously, with the wealth of information available these days, and the ease with which we can share that information, it's easy to let these things get spread around. However, consider the time and effort Daisy and Anna have put in to creating this content to provide to you and to others. It takes very little time for the end user to obtain and/or share this material, but it takes quite a bit more time for the creators of the material to plan it out, write it, edit it, collate it, and deliver it TO you, the end user!

With that in mind, if you have found this information useful, and we hope you have, please let others know about the content by directing them to purchase this book, or the online course version of the book, which includes videos and the opportunity for you to get feedback on your progress from the authors, by heading to Daisy's online learning website, https://www.performancepuppyabcs.com - thank you!

~ Anna and Daisy

PERFORMANCE PUPPY ABCs
www.performancepuppyabcs.com

Copyright © 2019, 2020 by Daisy Creative, LLC
Written and edited by Daisy Peel and Anna Hinze
ISBN 978-1-7362115-1-9

www.ingramcontent.com/pod-product-compliance
Lightning Source LLC
Chambersburg PA
CBHW051256110526
44589CB00025B/2845